Asian Resorts

Bhutan Indonesia Japan Laos Maldives Malaysia Taiwan Thailand UAE

photography & text by **Akihiko Seki**

TUTTLE PUBLISHING
Tokyo • Rutland, Vermont • Singapore

Published by Tuttle Publishing, an imprint of Periplus Editions (HK) Ltd., with editorial offices at 364 Innovation Drive, North Clarendon, Vermont 05759 USA and 61 Tai Seng Avenue, #02-12, Singapore 534167

ISBN: 978-0-8048-4055-2

Distributed by

North America, Latin America & Europe
Tuttle Publishing
364 Innovation Drive, North Clarendon
VT 05759-9436 USA
Tel: 1 (802) 773-8930; Fax: 1 (802) 773-6993
info@tuttlepublishing.com; www.tuttlepublishing.com

Japan
Tuttle Publishing
Yaekari Building, 3rd Floor, 5-4-12 Osaki,
Shinagawa-ku, Tokyo 141 0032
Tel: (81) 03 5437-0171; Fax: (81) 03 5437-0755
tuttle-sales@gol.com

Asia Pacific
Berkeley Books Pte. Ltd.
61 Tai Seng Avenue, #02-12, Singapore 534167
Tel: (65) 6280-1330; Fax: (65) 6280-6290
inquiries@periplus.com.sg; www.periplus.com

Indonesia
PT Java Books Indonesia
Kawasan Industri Pulogadung
Jl. Rawa Gelam IV No. 9, Jakarta 13930
Tel: (62) 21 4682-1088; Fax: (62) 21 461-0206
cs@javabooks.co.id

12 11 10 09   6 5 4 3 2 1

Printed in Singapore

Front endpaper: One & Only Reethi Rah, the Maldives (page 104).

Back endpaper: The Oberoi Lombok, Indonesia (page 63).

Page 1: Cocoa Island, the Maldives (page 96).

Page 2: The Oberoi Lombok, Indonesia (page 63).

Pages 4–5: Four Seasons Resort Langkawi, Malaysia (page 122).

Contents

SIMPLY THE BEST 009

Bhutan　　UMA PARO Paro 016

Indonesia　　AMANKILA Bali 022
AYANA RESORT & SPA Bali 028
BAGUS JATI HEALTH AND WELL-BEING RETREAT Bali 034
COMO SHAMBHALA ESTATE at BEGAWAN GIRI Bali 040
LOSARI COFFEE PLANTATION RESORT & SPA Magelang, Java 046
MIMPI RESORT MENJANGAN Bali 052
THE OBEROI BALI Bali 056
THE OBEROI LOMBOK Lombok 062
THE ROYAL PITA MAHA Bali 066

Japan　　GAJOEN & TENKUH-NO-MORI Kagoshima 072
GOSHO BESSHO Kobe 078
INN SEIRYUSO Shimoda 082
THALASSA SHIMA HOTEL & RESORT Toba 088

Laos　　MAISON SOUVANNAPHOUM Luang Prabang 092

Maldives　　COCOA ISLAND Makunufushi Island 096
KANUHURA Lhaviyani Atoll 100
ONE & ONLY REETHI RAH North Malé Atoll 104
THE RANIA EXPERIENCE Maafushi Island 110

Malaysia　　CAMERON HIGHLANDS RESORT Cameron Highlands 114
CARCOSA SERI NEGARA Kuala Lumpur 118
FOUR SEASONS RESORT LANGKAWI Langkawi 122
PANGKOR LAUT RESORT Perak 128
THE DATAI LANGKAWI Langkawi 132
THE MAGELLAN SUTERA Kota Kinabalu 136

Taiwan　　SPRING PARK URAI SPA & RESORT Taipei 140

Thailand　　ANANTARA GOLDEN TRIANGLE RESORT & SPA Chiang Rai 144
BAAN TALING NGAM RESORT & SPA Samui 148
BLUE CANYON COUNTRY CLUB Phuket 152
CHIVA-SOM INTERNATIONAL HEALTH RESORT Hua Hin 150
FOUR SEASONS RESORT CHIANG MAI Chiang Mai 160
MANDARIN ORIENTAL DHARA DHEVI Chiang Mai 166
RAYAVADEE Krabi 172
THE PENINSULA BANGKOK Bangkok 178
THE TONGSAI BAY Samui 182

UAE　　ONE & ONLY ROYAL MIRAGE Dubai 186

ACKNOWLEDGMENTS 192

Simply the Best

"I have the simplest of tastes, I am always satisfied with the best."
Oscar Wilde

Magnificent views, lavish living spaces, impeccable service–
nothing but the best is what today's top-tier resort-goers expect,
whether in a remote destination or a bustling city. Added to the list
are rich cultures, warm and friendly people, unspoiled beaches, private pools, decadent dining and full-service spas. Not surprisingly,
Asia's luxury resorts offer all these and more, having set the standard, years ago, for what the luxury traveler wants–and expects. From
a yoga resort in the hills of Bhutan to a stilted villa above a blue
lagoon in the Maldives, there is an unmatched range of luxurious
accommodations available in Asia to satisfy those looking to escape
and well as those in search of a one-of-a-kind experience. Beach
resorts, hill resorts, spa resorts, health resorts, golf resorts–there
is something for everyone. All the resorts showcased in this book
epitomize grandeur and opulence and inimitable Asian hospitality.
But what makes them really stand out, what makes them so irresist-
ible, even addictive, luring travelers back time and time again, is
the way in which all the modern-day taken-for-granted amenities
are packaged and presented in a veneer of unique local architecture
and culture. It is the fusion of the traditional and the contemporary
that is at the heart of the Asian resort appeal.

The Asian resorts covered here are scattered throughout a vast
area sandwiched between the Indian and Pacific Oceans, stretching from the United Arab Emirates in the west to Bhutan and the
Maldives in the center to Japan, Taiwan, Laos, Thailand, Malaysia

and Indonesia in the east. Most of the beachside and island resorts, for those who seek the best beaches and dive spots, are located along a broad band straddling the equator, from the Maldives in the middle of the Indian Ocean to the vast Indonesian archipelago bordering the Pacific Ocean. Blessed with a tropical climate, it is the landscape of these idyllic getaways in the Maldivian archipelago, the west coast islands of Malaysia, Phuket and Koh Samui in Thailand and the island of Bali in Indonesia that greets and entrances the first-time visitor—and the returnee: swaying palms, lush green foliage, pristine powdery white beaches, crystal-clear azure waters, exotic cultures and friendly people.

All of these resorts are designed to cope with life in the tropics, with its bright sunlight, high humidity and monsoon rains. All draw on and reinterpret rich and diverse local architectural styles to create resorts suitable for modern living, and all use traditional materials—bamboo, *alang-alang* grass thatching, wood, stone and slate—in their architecture to create spaces that are cool and do not absorb the intense heat. Many of the resorts are light and breezy, with open areas and high roof spaces designed to maximize natural ventilation. Broad verandahs, screened patios, cool court-yards and steeply pitched roofs with wide eaves and deep overhangs provide shade. The use of timber discourages heat from entering, and window louvers and other similar devices filter light. All these delightful qualities add to the comfort, tranquility and beauty of the buildings. Some of the most enchanting tropical resorts featured here are set over water and accessed by boardwalks. Others cling to the sides of steep cliffs. Most have contemporary spatial organizations, yet successfully combine traditional features with modern-day needs and tastes.

In the interior design of these tropical resorts, guests are treated to a showcase of the "Asian look." Wooden floors made of teak or other local hardwoods create a feeling of underfoot luxury, while patterned ceramic tiles or marble slabs are cool to the touch in bathrooms and public areas.

The furniture, furnishings, arts and crafts that contribute to the beautiful interiors illustrate how the talents of local crafts people–recipients of traditional skills passed down through the generations–have been harnessed to create a wide variety of decorative items. Vibrant handwoven bed and table runners, stunning wall hangings and intricately carved wooden screens imbue a sense of place and authenticity and add touches of color to otherwise muted tones. Much of the furniture, predominantly of teak, represents a melding of East and West, a reinterpretation of influences, be they Asian or European, through an innate sensitivity to Asian culture. Particularly luxurious are the resorts' bathrooms. Spacious sanctuaries that harness design possibilities using the rich array of raw materials available in Asia, many sport tubs for two looking out to private water-filled courtyards and luxuriant foliage. Others take the essence of the tropical river bath and adapt it to the Western needs of privacy and luxury with walled, open-to-the sky bathing places.

Life in the tropics has always been about living out of doors. Most of the beachside and island resorts in this book, as well as the hill resorts in the tropical uplands of South-east Asia, highlight the relationship of the architecture to nature and blend harmoniously into their natural surroundings. Palm trees predominate on the islands of the Maldives, but lushly landscaped gardens, often terraced, form an integral part of most other tropical properties, merging the dwellings with their surroundings, blurring the distinction between the interior and the exterior, and providing relief from the heat and glare. An artful blend of exotic plants and trees is invariably interspersed with meandering pathways, pools, fountains, streams, bridges, lichen-clad terracotta pots, sandstone bas-reliefs and stone and wood statuary. Gardens are often set against a backdrop of mist-shrouded rain forest or towering limestone cliffs. In northern Thailand, working rice paddies form an innovative and fascinating part of the landscaping, while in upland Indonesia and Malaysia tea and coffee plantations contribute to stunning vistas. Whatever

their location, the gardens of all the resorts offer delights not just with their colors, forms, textures and compositional arrangements, but also through their fragrances and essentially contemplative qualities.

In the cooler climes of Bhutan, Japan, Taiwan and Korea, splendid views of misty forested mountains, cultivated plains and settlements, gurgling rivers and steaming hot springs soothe the senses. Nature treks, hiking and mountain biking are on offer for the physically active. Here, too, the focus is on health and well-being and a resort's spa, often designed around mineral hot springs, is generally its reason for being. Spas have also become a significant feature of the tropical resorts of the equatorial belt, offering an extensive menu of authentic massages, pampering body treatments and other wellness therapies in beautifully appointed open-air pavilions or indoor rooms. Most integrate traditional Asian medicinal practices, particularly Ayurvedic practices, with Western philosophies to produce a wide array of slimming, detoxification and revitalizing therapies, and most employ exclusively designed spa products based on the healing properties of local aromatic ingredients. Spiritual and holistic treatments like yoga, reiki and meditation classes conducted in serene landscaped settings are a popular option. Some spas offer new and quirky treatments, such as crystal and gem therapy.

Attention to all things culinary is also important in Asia and many of the resorts' restaurants focus on dishes prepared with local ingredients, some grown organically on the premises. Produce fresh from the sea is a feature of the restaurants at beachside and island resorts. At some resorts, guests, including an increasing number of die-hard "foodies," can also take cooking classes and learn about the local culture through the dishes—after they have visited the local market to help purchase the ingredients.

The hospitality industry in Asia not only offers a wide range of luxury resort options for the affluent tourist but also the opportunity to absorb Asia's rich cultural heritage and a huge array of outdoor activities suited to the warm,

tropical climate. Local events and festivities are complemented by cultural visits to local markets, crafts villages, museums, temples and tribal settlements. For those who love the sea, the pristine beach resorts in the Maldives, Malaysia, Thailand and Indonesia that are highlighted in this book have some of the finest beaches and dive spots in the world. The whole gamut of water activities is available for both the novice and the experienced adventurer—surfing, snorkeling, waterskiing, parasailing, kayaking, scuba diving, high-speed rafting and game fishing. Complementing the sea, a magnificent swimming pool—or often pools—usually with a dramatic infinity edge, is invariably a focus of Asian resorts. Whether it is a luxurious resort inspired by sun, sea and sand or a cool-clime resort that capitalizes on its unusual mountain or river setting, this book contains a visual feast of the best Asian-inspired resort experiences.

Opposite: Lushly landscaped gardens at Rayavadee, Krabi, Thailand.
Top: Yoga amidst the rice paddies at the Four Seasons Resort, Chiang Mai, Thailand.

Above: A sweeping view of the Paro Valley from the hillside Uma Paro resort.

Left: The snow-clad Himalayas viewed from the pass at 12,500 feet (3,800 meters) above sea level.

Opposite: The staff at Uma Paro wear charming traditional Bhutanese costumes.

Uma Paro Bhutan

Located in one of the most isolated and beautiful corners of the world, the tiny and remote Himalayan kingdom of Bhutan, Uma Paro, opened in 2004, is a luxury romantic getaway like no other. Just 10 minutes from Bhutan's only airport, the hotel, perched amidst blue pine forest overlooking the Paro Valley, enjoys magnificent views of the peaks above and the rice paddies, wheat fields, streams, scattered settlements, temples and monasteries below. The hotel's stunning location, combined with its strong Buddhist traditions, creates a serene and, for many, spiritual experience.

The heart of the hotel, the former home of a Bhutanese nobleman, is a three-story structure in vernacular style, with a flat roof, stark white stucco walls and painted wood window borders. Inside, low timber-beamed ceilings and white walls vividly painted by local artists with traditional motifs combine with *bukhari* stoves, textile carpets and cushioned seating to exude a charm reminiscent of a country home. Nine villas, crafted by traditionally trained Bhutanese artisans, with Zen-inspired interiors containing luxury amenities such as private therapy suites, are scattered around the 38-acre (15-hectare) wooded hillside site and are accessible by golf buggy.

In the typically Bhutanese circular dining room, named appropriately Bukhari after the centrally placed fireplace that warms the room, broad windows allow splendid views of the dense pine forest. The menu features traditional Bhutanese offerings such as dried local pork and hearty soups made from handmade noodles, as well as contemporary interpretations of neighboring cuisines, including Indian dishes from the charcoal tandoor oven.

The holistic heart of Uma Paro–and the main reason for its existence–is the Como Shambhala Retreat. The emphasis at its treatment and steam rooms, gym and indoor pool–with outdoor sundeck–is less on beauty than on yoga, massage and Ayurvedic medicine as staff strive to offer physical as well as spiritual wellness. For physical adventure, the hotel offers overnight trekking and camping expeditions, day walks, mountain biking, archery and rafting.

Left: A traditional *bukhari* fireplace in one of the villas set against a wall decorated with Bhutanese paintings.
Top: Paintings on ceilings and walls are an attractive feature at the resort.
Right: Prayer bells at one of the hillside temples in the vicinity of the resort.

Address: Uma Paro
PO Box 222, Paro, Bhutan.
Tel: +975 8 271 597
Fax: +975 8 271 513
E-mail: info.paro@uma.como.bz
Website: www.uma.como.bz

Above: The three-story main building in vernacular style.
Below: The resort's well-equipped gym and yoga studio overlook the Paro Valley.
Opposite top: A wooden tub in the four-room spa.
Opposite bottom left: The view from a villa terrace.
Opposite bottom right: A butler delivers room service.

Above: The signature three-tiered blue-tiled pool sits dramatically on the side of the cliff just below the lobby.
Opposite: Charming little dancing girls add to the allure of the resort.

Amankila Bali

An hour's drive from Bali's international airport at Denpasar, Amankila is the ultimate luxury retreat for romantic, spiritual, cultural and activity pursuits. Set on a beachfront plateau between two headlands above the Lombok Strait near the village of Manggis on the east coast of Bali, Amankila, meaning "peaceful hill," enjoys stunning views of the sparkling sea and coastline and exclusive access to an idyllic, crescent-shaped beach. Rearing up behind, the volcanic Mount Agung, revered by the Balinese as a home of the gods, towers over the resort and its seaside setting. Cultural excursions to nearby temples, craft villages and ancient water palaces, and a host of physical activities ranging from diving to mountain biking, contribute to an unforgettable, all-round Amankila resort experience.

Most people who come to the resort, however, are happy to sit, soak and sun. The hallmark of Amankila is a three-tiered infinity pool, reminiscent of terraced rice paddies, which cascades down from the frangipani-bordered reception lobby toward the shore. Lined with loungers and *alang-alang* grass-thatched *balé* pavilions, the pool is an ideal setting for dining or simply gazing at the sea. At the base of the cliff, set back from the beach, a 134-foot (41-meter)-long lap pool nestled among swaying coconut palms is the centerpiece of the Beach Club. Guests can also enjoy traditional Balinese massage and beauty treatments in the club's wooden massage pavilions or yoga classes under the palms.

Above: A mesmerizing view of the private pool and the Lombok Strait beyond from the Indrakila Suite.
Right: At the Beach Club, two teakwood massage tables are hidden away in a grove of coconut palms and flowering shrubs.
Below: The villas' spacious outdoor terraces are furnished with daybeds and dining furniture.

Halfway up the tree-clothed hill, and blending seamlessly with the verdant surroundings, 34 freestanding suites radiate out from the main building in two deep crescents. Built in the ubiquitous Balinese style of wooden structure topped by round *alang-alang* thatched roof, each suite has an outdoor terrace furnished with a large daybed with comfy pillows and bolsters for lounging and a table and chairs for private dining, a deep soaking tub looking out over a miniature manicured garden and other top-of-the-range amenities. Most villas enjoy views of the sea. A mesh of raised walkways links the villas to the restaurants, swimming pools and other public areas.

Above: Amankila's signature three-tiered infinity-edge swimming pool echoes Bali's terraced rice paddies.

Opposite top left: A small selection of natural herbal products.

Opposite top right and below, this page above and left: Views of the panoramically endowed freestanding Kilasari Suite, with its spacious outdoor terrace, private pool and luxuriously appointed bathroom.

Address: Amankila
Manggis, Bali
Indonesia
Tel: +62 363 41333
Fax: +62 363 41555
E-mail: amankila@amanresorts.com
Website: www.amanresorts.com

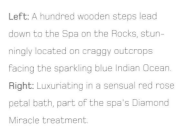

Left: A hundred wooden steps lead down to the Spa on the Rocks, stunningly located on craggy outcrops facing the sparkling blue Indian Ocean. **Right:** Luxuriating in a sensual red rose petal bath, part of the spa's Diamond Miracle treatment.

AYANA Resort & Spa

Dramatically perched on a bluff overlooking the Indian Ocean at the southwestern tip of Bali, the AYANA Resort & Spa (formerly the Ritz-Carlton Bali) more than lives up to its name—Ayana means "place of refuge" in Sanskrit—despite its location a mere 6 miles (10 km) from bustling Denpasar and Ngurah Rai International Airport. Some 70 percent of the 192-acre (77-hectare) site is used to accommodate business conferences, wedding parties, spa junkies and hallmark romantics. A state-of-the-art business conference center for 800 and a clifftop wedding atrium are among the facilities, the latter particularly popular with Japanese guests. Buggy highways lined with brightly blooming bougainvillea and fragrant frangipani link the 368 luxuriously appointed guest rooms, including 78 private villas and 16 suites, which overlook some of the island's finest coastline. Staircases, promenades, fountains and statuary spread out from the main four-story building and reception, cascading down to the beach.

But it is the AYANA's Spa on the Rocks, opened in 2006, that draws most attention. Comprising two private treatment villas nestled on rocks amidst the ocean, it adjoins the Thermes Marins Bali Spa, which includes not only the largest Thalasso (seawater) therapy facility in Asia but its seawater-filled aquatonic exercise pool is one of the

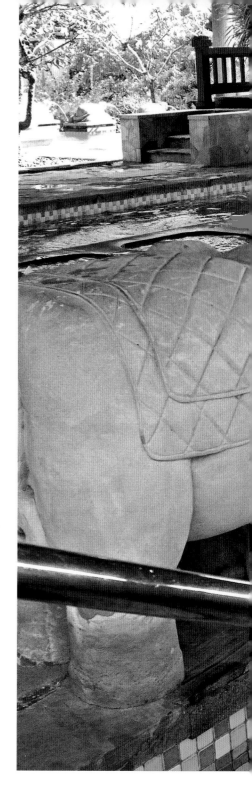

most entertaining around. The Ocean Beach Pool at the bottom of the cliff, filled with filtered seawater pumped up from the bay, is an alternative to a swim in the sea at Kubu beach.

Restaurant choices at AYANA include Balinese, Japanese and Mediterranean cafés and a superb seafood grill that overlooks crashing waves and incredible sunsets.

Opposite top and bottom: An enticing bedroom and a tub for two in front of picture windows in one of the cliff villas, set in a private courtyard. **Above:** The entertaining seawater-filled aqua-tonic exercise pool and spa.

Top: Candle-lit dinners on the pier are a romantic option.
Right: The resort's thatch-roofed garden villas are nestled within manicured gardens abloom with brilliant bougainvillea and frangipani.

Above: A therapeutic massage with oils bound with elements of silk and pearl is part of the ultra-luxurious Diamond Miracle treatment at the Spa on the Rocks.

Below: The sedate seawater-filled Ocean Beach Pool is a contrast to the rock-studded sea below where guests can enjoy swimming at low tide.

Address: AYANA Resort & Spa
Jl. Karang Mas Sejahtera
Jimbaran, Bali, Indonesia
Tel: +62 361 702222
Fax: +62 361 701555
E-mail: reservation@ayanaresort.com
Website: www.ayanaresort.com

Bagus Jati Retreat Bali

Bagus Jati, literally "good teakwood" in Indonesian but metaphorically "strength
of character" in Balinese, is a small health and well-being retreat set in 12 acres
(5 hectares) of hillside gardens amidst lush tropical forests in the mountains of Bali,
about 30 minutes' drive north from Ubud, the island's cultural and artistic center.
The brainchild of former travel agent and hotelier Bagus Sudibya, Bagus Jati is
distinguished from most other spas by its natural "green" setting (cultivated beds
of herbs and organic vegetables, flowering shrubs and fruiting trees, and grassed
terraces fill every inch of space between the buildings) and its philosophy (manag-
ing stress through "lifestyle training"). Local farmers helped to develop the retreat
and continue to maintain it.

Bagus Jati focuses on the natural in its architecture as well as its therapies.
Guests have a choice of eight circular deluxe spa villas, each with a private whirlpool,
treatment room and balcony, or ten square superior villas, all designed to integrate

Opposite top: The circular timber yoga and meditation pavilion, built within a bamboo forest, is an exquisite and inspirational setting.
Opposite bottom: The resort's hand-hewn ochre swimming pool is filled with warmed spring water.
Above and right: Nature is all-encompassing at Bagus Jati, from the hillside botanical gardens to the mist-covered tropical forest.

Above: The circular style of the villas and other buildings is based on early primitive village dwellings as well as the ancient chakra principle concerning whorls of energy.

Left: A pair of decorative Javanese *loro blonyo* dolls guarantee couples a long life together.

Right: Mind-soothing Ayurvedic *shirodhara* (oil therapy).

Above: Produce grown on the property
is used in spa treatments and cuisine.
Below: One of the exquisitely furnished
spa villas equipped with private Jacuzzi
and spa treatment facilities.

Address: Bagus Jati Health & Well-Being Retreat

Bandar Jati, Desa Sebatu

Kecamatan, Tegallalang

Ubud, Gianyar

Bali 80572, Indonesia

Tel: +62 361 978 885/+62 361 901 888

E-mail: info@bagusjati.com

Website: www.bagusjati.com

Above: The setting for the Balinese court-inspired Sejati ("Real Life") signature treatment.

Below: Trained therapists come from the surrounding villages.

Left: Stone pavers lead to a villa.
Below: Bagus Jati focuses on the natural in both its spa architecture and therapies.
Right: Water spurts from gargoyles into the main pool.

the spa with the natural surroundings. Broad windows allow unfettered views of the mountains, valleys and lush tropical floral and fauna. A complete health and well-being center and a gourmet restaurant offering specially prepared spa cuisine contribute to the timeless wisdom of traditional healing. Adventure tours, garden or jungle walks and cooking classes form part of educational programs.

The preparations used at Bagus Jati to refresh and rejuvenate the body and mind are all based on the healing properties of local aromatic ingredients such as lemongrass, galangal, turmeric root, cinnamon bark and vanilla pods, all grown on the premises, handpicked and ground. Banana leaf body wraps utilizing green pandanus leaf scrubs, nutritious body polishes and acupressure massages are among the renewal treatments. Innovative spa rituals merge Vichy rain showers with pure volcanic mud from the nearby isalnd of Lombok and mind-soothing Ayurvedic oil therapy.

Above: Wanakasa (Forest in the Mist) Residence
stands sentinel over tall trees and dense foliage.
Opposite top: A *kecak* (monkey dance) performance.
Opposite bottom: The three-walled Sukma Taru
(Spirit Tree), a private villa, overlooks an infinity pool.

Como Shambhala Estate

Water is at the heart of the Como Shambhala Estate, an award-winning residential wellness retreat and the flagship of Como Shambhala, staggered up the steep slopes of the Ayung River gorge, a 20-minute drive from Ubud, Bali's cultural center. The focus of the 22-acre (9-hectare) property are a trio of streams, a sacred natural spring revered for its healing properties, and a cluster of rock pools that have been harnessed into a variety of swimming, plunge and free-form pools, whirlpools and outdoor showers, all providing the water and hydrotherapy that are key elements in Como Shambhala's healing processes.

The Estate, opened in 2005, occupies the former property of Begawan Giri, a retreat developed by an English couple, Bradley and Deborah Gardner, who bought the site in 1989, built five grand residences and planted 2,000 hardwood trees. Now billing itself "A Retreat for Change," the Como Shambhala Estate offers comprehensive lifestyle as well as healing programs tailored to anyone in need of a recharge—physically, spiritually or emotionally. For the purification-inclined, the Estate's Kudus House and Glow restaurants serve delicious, healthy food made with organic, locally sourced ingredients. Meals can be tailored to suit individual needs.

Left: A deluxe suite at Tirta-Ening (Clear Water) Residence is furnished with old-world antique charm.
Right: A stylized stone turtle watches over a lush gully.
Below: The dramatic infinity-edge pool at Wanakasa appears to float above the surrounding treetops.

Above: Tejasuara (Sound of Fire) Residence, inspired by the island of Sumba, comprises four sturdy thatch-roofed suites constructed of Sumban stone, arrayed around a central pool. The suites are filled with fascinating tribal artifacts and bamboo beds.

Bottom: A Como Shambhala masseuse at work at the private contemporary-style Vasudhara retreat villa.

The accommodations at the Como Shambhala Estate are among the most private, spacious and luxurious of their kind in the holistic pursuit of taking care of mind, body and spirit. Five pagoda-style thematic Residences (Fire, Water, Wind, Forest and Earth), made from local stone, woods and *alang-alang* grass thatching in a mix of contemporary design and indigenous detailing, are scattered among sun-filtered, jade-green clearings. Each Residence has four or five suites furnished with old-world antique charm, and each shares a large living room and chaise-surrounded infinity-edge swimming pool. For those seeking more privacy, there are stand-alone private villas, garden villas and retreat villas with assorted living spaces, private pools and spa rooms and state-of-the-art amenities. A small army of life coaches, energy healers, yoga masters, activity guides and nutritionists help guests "make informed life changes" in quest of better health in an environment that combines wilderness and refinement.

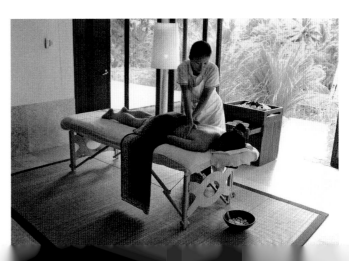

Address: Como Shambhala Estate Begawan Giri
PO Box 54, Ubud
Gianyar 80571
Bali, Indonesia
Tel: +62 361 978 888
Fax: +62 361 978 889
E-mail: info@comoshambhala.bz
Website: www.comoshambhala.bz

Left: The reception area at Como Shambhala provides a soothng glimpse of what is in store for guests at this award-winning holistic retreat.

Opposite bottom left: The décor of the five suites at the shingle-roofed Wanakasa is light and contemporary.

Opposite bottom right: The exotic menus at the retreat's two restaurants can be tailored to any dietary whim.

Right: The stunning floating pool pavilion at the Zen-inspired Tirta-Ening.

Below: A bath at Wanakasa carved from Sumban stone.

Losari Coffee Plantation

Sprawling across 55 acres (22 hectares) in the volcanic highlands above Magelang on Indonesia's main island of Java is the Losari Coffee Plantation Resort & Spa, an old-world coffee plantation turned unique boutique villa retreat. Losari, which means "essence of trees" in Javanese, is a working plantation with fields of *Robusta javanensis* coffee growing in the shadow of eight volcanoes, its own "ring of fire," including the still-active Mount Merapi. A great inland plantation during Indonesia's colonial years, then abandoned to dereliction in the forests of Central Java, Losari has been restored to its former glory—and much more—by Italian biologist Gabriella Teggia, one of the founders of the Amandari resort in Bali. She bought the property in 1992 and devoted a ten-year labor of love to rejuvenating the plantation as well as creating a deluxe resort and spa. Both provide special glimpses into the past.

The heart of the property is an old plantation house on a hillock that was built originally in 1828 and now forms the Club House. Teggia commissioned two Italian architects, brothers, to restore the main house and gardens. They added imposing white columns and an expansive wraparound verandah, where breakfast, informal lunches and high tea are served. Public areas

Above: The original Dutch plantation house.

Opposite top: The working coffee plantation.

Opposite bottom: Some of the volcanoes encircling the resort viewed from the garden.

Top: The old-style mood of the resort extends to the bedrooms.
Above: *Robusta javanensis* beans.
Opposite top left: Stunning emerald-sheened rice terraces.
Opposite top right: Private balconies overlook rain forests.
Opposite bottom: The Losari Spa blends ancient Javanese beauty treatments with yoga and Turkish-style steam rooms.

within the plantation house include a lounge, library and music room furnished in the Dutch colonial style with wood-and-rattan rocking chairs, comfortable loungers and armoires. A stone path lined with terracotta planters leads to the main entrance, while a well-tended lawn complete with croquet hoops surrounds the house.

Within the grounds of the plantation are 26 all-suite villas, situated so as to take in the stunning volcano views. Formed from traditional Javanese houses earmarked for destruction which Teggia found, bought, had dismantled and transported to Losari and reassembled, the villas comprise an eclectic mix of Javanese architectural styles, some with soaring hipped *joglo*-style tiled roofs, others with the five-ridged hipped *limasan* style-roof. The interiors are roomy and romantic and tastefully decorated with Javan and other antiques. Similarly, old open-sided pavilions (*pendopo*) sourced from around Java constitute the bar, restaurant and gamelan stage.

Losari's purpose-built spa features Indonesian herbal treatments and traditional beauty recipes from the royal palace of Yogyakarta as well as Asia's only authentic Turkish steam bath, the Hamam. For the more energetic, there are plantation tours, dawn trips to Borobodur and other temples, sightseeing and shopping trips to Semarang, Yogyakarta and Surakarta, and volcano climbing and trekking.

Left and above: Sampling *jamu*, Java's traditional energy drink, made here from tree sap, honey and fragrant herbs.
Below: Guest accommodation in a re-stored *joglo*-style roofed house.

Above: Yoga and stretching exercises are offered for early morning risers near the fish pond.

Right: Apart from producing 20 tons of coffee each year, the plantation also yields practically everything served at the table, including bananas, peanuts amd coconuts and the spiky, foul-smelling durian fruit shown here.

Address: Losari Coffee Plantation Resort & Spa Desa Losari, Grabag, PO Box 108, Magelang 596100, Central Java, Indonesia.
Tel: +62 298 596 333
Fax: +62 298 592 696
E-mail: info@losaricoffeeplantation.com
Website: www.losaricoffeeplantation.com

Mimpi Resort Menjangan Bali

Tucked away on the shores of the lagoon-like Banyuwedang Bay on Bali's northwest coast, Mimpi Resort is ideally located to discover the best of Bali, both underwater and on land. Blessed not only with close proximity to Menjangan Island, one of Bali's best-known diving spots, and to the neighboring Bali Barat National Park with its extraordinary flora and fauna, Mimpi Resort is also endowed with abundant natural hot springs throughout its mangrove-bordered grounds.

Taking advantage of this mineral-rich natural resource, the resort is designed along the lines of a traditional Balinese village, with 24 walled courtyard villas and 30 terraced patio rooms. The courtyard villas, built in wood with thatched roofs, are accessed through traditional roofed Balinese doorways. Within each walled compound is a hot spring tub. Six of the villas have dipping pools built from natural blue stone filled with thermal waters. The open-to-sky garden bathrooms in the patio rooms and

the lush greenery viewed from the spacious verandahs provide a cool, green ambience. An alternative is the natural hot spring pool set in the beautifully landscaped gardens in front of the patio rooms. Another large thermal pool overlooking the bay caters to all guests.

The Sunset Restaurant and bar float on the quiet waters of the bay, open to cooling sea breezes and the changing colors of the evening sky.

A fully equipped dive center, complete with expert instructors, caters to beginner as well as experienced divers. For non-divers, other water sport options include snorkeling, kayaking and sea biking.

After an active day, water sport enthusiasts can soak in one of the resort's hot springs or enjoy a variety of treatments at the spa. Traditional and aromatherapy massages and body scrubs employing natural ingredients are guaranteed to rejuvenate both mind and body.

Left: A shady gazebo, a natural stone hot spring tub and a dipping pool are the ultimate in luxury at this walled villa.
Top: The Sunset Restaurant overlooks the quiet waters of the bay by day and stunning sunsets by night.
Below: Traditional massage at a courtyard villa set in a tropical garden paradise.

Top: From the circular communal hot spring pool, guests can enjoy a magnificent view of the bay and the surrounding mangroves.

Right: Frangipani blossoms float in a hot spring tub in a secluded courtyard villa.

Address: Mimpi Resort Menjangan Banyuwedang, 81155 Buleleng Bali, Indonesia
Tel: +63 362 94497
Fax: +63 363 94498
E-mail: menjangan@mimpi.com
Website: www.mimpi.com

Right: A figure carved from volcanic sandstone welcomes guests.
Bottom: The thatch-roofed entrance gate to one of the luxury villas.
Opposite: Teak, bamboo and rattan dominate in the villa interiors.

The Oberoi Bali

Considering its location right on Seminyak Beach, not far from the hustle and bustle of Kuta on Bali's southwest coast, The Oberoi offers a surprisingly peaceful setting and remains one of Bali's most popular luxury hotels for rest and relaxation. Huge seafront grounds–the resort is set amidst 15 acres (6 hectares) of tranquil gardens–and a 550-yard (500-meter) beachfront bordering the Indian Ocean contribute to the seclusion and serenity of the resort, which dates from 1978, making it one of the first.

The luxurious accommodations at the hotel complement its stunning natural setting. Ranging from villa suites set behind coral stone walls for privacy, with swimming pools, courtyards, rock pools and pavilions for alfresco dining, to lanai rooms featuring private verandahs and sunken tubs in unique garden bathrooms, every modern convenience is available to guests. The interiors successfully combine the traditional and the modern, the old and the new, the raw and the finished. Balinese teak furniture dominates, offset by an eclectic mix of oversized cane sofas and chairs, stuffed cushions and woven rugs.

Meandering paths formed of hexagonal pavers sheltered by frangipani and banyan trees lead through the gardens to the pool and other public facilities. The pool at The Oberoi is situated very close to the sea, seemingly joined with the crashing waves. Brightly hued umbrellas offer shelter from the blistering sun. Guests can enjoy themed buffet dinners at the Ampitheater, adjacent to the beach, accompanied by Balinese dance performances, light meals under trees on the beach, or fine dining in the hotel's Balinese pavilion.

For true indulgence, guests can opt for the Javanese bathing ritual at The Oberoi Spa managed by Banyan Tree.

Left: Hexagonal pavers lead the way to the villas.
Opposite bottom: A Balinese Hindu god adds color and interest to the gardens.
Below: An elaborately carved and gilded doorway set into a coral stone wall in the reception area.
Right: A soothing massage at a luxury pool villa.
Right bottom: Guests can enjoy Balinese dancing at the open-air amphitheater.

Above: The inviting swimming pool, adjacent to Seminyak Beach.
Right: Yoga on one of Bali's most beautiful beaches in front of the hotel.

Below: Sunset at the Frangipani Café, located on the beachfront.

Bottom left: Another carved statue from the Hindu pantheon of gods.

Address: The Oberoi Bali
Seminyak Beach, Jalan Laksmana
PO Box 3351, Denpasar 80033
Bali, Indonesia
Tel: +62 361 730 361
Fax: +62 361 730 791
E-mail: gm@theoberoi-bali.com
Website: www.oberoibali.com

The Oberoi Lombok

The island of Lombok, located 40 miles (65 km) due east of Bali and accessible by air or sea (speedboat, catamaran or public ferry), is becoming increasingly popular as a holiday destination for its white, sandy beaches in quieter settings, the unique culture of its Sasak people and its water sports and eco adventures. There is no better place from which to enjoy these attractions than The Oberoi, isolated on a head-land of the small but perfect Medana Beach, a 45-minute drive northwest of the capital Mataram and its airport, Selaparang. On a clear day, Mount Agung in Bali can be seen rearing its head across the Lombok Strait.

Fifty elegant thatched-roof villas and terraced pavilions with expansive, shaded patios offering either garden or ocean views, are scattered around 24 acres (10 hectares) of mani-cured lawns dotted with palms and colorful garden beds. A generous use of teak in the rooms, richly woven carpets and Indonesian artifacts add local character. Sunken baths set in private pink-tinged walled gardens are the ultimate in luxury. Throughout the property there is a prevailing sense of peace and solitude, the silence broken only by the sound of crashing waves and the chirping of birds.

A splendid infinity pool is the main focus at The Oberoi, its overflowing edge optically meeting the shimmering blue

sea beyond. From the covered sun loungers and open-sided pavilions lining the half moon-shaped pool, itself fringed by tall, curving palms, the huge expanse of ocean and the horizon are mesmerizing, second only to the spectacular sunsets. The sound and sight of surf is ever present and wave watching is a favorite and relaxing pastime. For the more active, the nearby Gili Islands, reached by a short boat ride from the hotel's Beach Club, set at the end of a picturesque jetty, offer beautiful clear waters with dazzling coral gardens and tropical fish. Expert tutors are on hand for those who want to try their hand at a variety of water sports.

Also ocean-inspired are the hotel's beach- and poolside restaurants and cafés and spa. The Oberoi Spa, managed by Banyan Tree, offers a wide range of international standard massages and other treatments synonymous with the magic and mystery of Indonesia.

Opposite: Palm trees and mirror pools set the scene at this quiet retreat.
Top: Sunset over the main pool.
Left: The spacious bedrooms are outfitted with teakwood furnishings and all modern conveniences.
Below: Horses are the main form of transportation in Lombok's villages.

Address: The Oberoi Lombok
Medana Beach, Tanjung
Mataram 83001, Lombok, Indonesia
Tel: +62 370 63 8444
Fax: +62 370 63 2496
E-mail: Gm.Toli@oberoihotels.com
Website: www.oberoilomok.com

The Royal Pita Maha Ubud

Owned, built and managed by Ubud's royal family, the Royal Pita Maha, opened in 2006, is a landscaped jewel, a quiet and secluded sanctuary etched into the side of the Campuhan valley overlooking the scenic Ayung River gorge in Ubud, Bali's cultural heartland. It is a mere one-hour drive from Bali's Ngurah Rai International Airport at Denpasar. At the Royal Pita Maha, the landscape in all its glory takes center stage. From most parts of the resort, a celestial vista of lush rice terraces, coconut palms, carefully tended cascading gardens and river gorge greets the eyes. It is an uplifting natural environment, an ideal place for peaceful contemplation. The experience is furthered by a focus on Bali's artistic heritage, with interactive classes in dance, music, painting, woodcarving, cooking and fruit carving and nightly performances of the best of Bali's classic dances. An adventure program of bird watching, trekking, whitewater rafting and cycling caters to the more activity-oriented, while an inspired range of excursions to nearby Ubud and its environs—local museums, artists' studios, galleries, temples, cultural performances and markets—offer culture to religion experiences.

Accommodations at the Royal Pita Maha are both ecologically sound and culturally appropriate to their setting. No effort has been spared by the owners in providing top-of-the-range comfort, services and amenities, and throughout there is an attention to detail that will delight any discerning guest. Built along the lines of an intimate Balinese village in the hills, the property comprises 41 pool villas commanding breathtaking views of verdant valley greenery, 10 healing villas surrounded by a riverside organic farm, and a royal villa, a luxurious three-level dwelling replicating the extravagance of a Balinese palace and featuring an intimate wedding chapel, two pavilion bedrooms and a garden courtyard. Every villa at this luxury resort comes with a

balcony, private garden and swimming pool and each is tastefully appointed with natural materials while harnessing light
and air flows in the rooms. Two terrace restaurants serving both
Asian and Western cuisine, two lounge bars, two free-form public
swimming pools, a spring water lagoon, a sauna and whirlpools,
a special yoga practice space and a serene meditation pavilion by
the river exemplify a Bali resort at its best. The Royal Pita Maha
is indeed a place to be pampered, a place of healing, reflection,
contemplation, meditation and serenity.

Of special architectural interest at the resort is the Royal
Convention House, set within a walled Balinese-style compound
on the crown of a hill. The compound houses a number of striking
traditional structures, including walls and gateways encrusted
with ornately carved bas-reliefs, open-sided pavilions and an
open-air stage. The custom-designed convention facilities include
two spacious meeting halls with tiered seating, the larger Gedong
House and the smaller Loji House, as well as meeting rooms.

Whether taking in vertiginous views over the valley, practicing
yoga by the river, imbibing tropical cocktails on the terrace, or
simply luxuriating in the near silence, a stay at the Royal Maha
Pita is not only a beguiling but also an exhilarating experience.

Opposite top: The resort's 10 healing villas are surrounded by a riverside organic farm.

Opposite bottom: The striking two-level restaurant, supported by huge wooden pillars, serves both Asian and Western specialties.

Above: Bedrooms in the pool villas are decorated in Balinese style with bamboo, teak and artwork.

Left: The picturesque holy spring.

Pages 70–71: A dramatic infinity-edge swimming pool, part of the amenities at each of the pool villas.

Address: The Royal Pita Maha
Desa Kedewatan, PO Box 198,
Ubud 80571, Bali, Indonesia
Tel: +62 361 980 022
Fax: +62 361 980 011
E-mail: sales@pitamaharesorts-bali.com
Website: www.royalpitamaha-bali.com

Gajoen & Tenkuh-no-Mori

Along the scenic west coast of Japan's southernmost main island, Kyushu, at Gajoen, about 15 minutes' drive north of Kagoshima Airport, are two amazing hideaways for the jaded–a picturesque hamlet simply called Gajoen and a nearby stunning hilltop forest haven called Tenkuh-no-Mori ("Forest of Heaven"). Situated in a rocky gorge just above the gurgling Amori River in 100 acres (40 hectares) of forest overlooking mountains, and drawing healing waters from the sulphur- and iron-rich hot spring resort of Myoken, Gajoen is probably the most highly sought after *onsen ryokan* (spa inn) in all of Japan. A 10-minute drive away, the smaller and even more exclusive retreat of Tenkuh-no-Mori, opened in December 2004, overlooks the enchanting Kirishima Mountains, offering a view perhaps without equal in all of Japan. A wonderful rustic sensibility prevails at both places.

Both retreats are the brainchild of former banker Tateo Tajima and his wife Etsuko. Quitting his humdrum job at a local bank in 1970, Tateo took over a small inn owned and managed by his mother. He sourced, relocated and reassembled thatched-roof houses, played the role of carpenter and plasterer, cleared forest with a bulldozer, planted bamboo, flowers and vegetables, laid down stone walkways and fashioned

Above: Guests at Gajoen share the stone walk-
ways with pecking and strutting chickens.
Opposite top: Clouds of steam billow into the air
at the small communal hot bath near the river at
Gajoen, concealed by a bamboo screen.
Opposite bottom: The private hot spring bath in
the Kaze cottage at Gajoen.
Right: Organic farm-fresh dinners are served
Japanese style in guests' cottages at Gajoen, on
a low table with a thick blanket-like covering.

Above and opposite bottom: The Hanachiru Sato villa at Tenkuh-no-Mori offers both breathtaking views of the mist-shrouded Kirishima Mountains and a wonderfully invigorating environment for yoga. All five villas at the retreat are elegantly simple yet luxurious, with huge outdoor decks inset with hot tubs.
Right: Guests can order sumptuous picnic lunches at Tenkuh-no-Mori.

outdoor bathtubs, all in the quest to return to a quintessential rural Japanese farming community of the 1920s—a pure earth, the transcendent peace of having fewer things and a heightened sense of the simplistic beauty of nature's rhythms.

There are only 10 thatched- or terracotta-roofed cottages at Gajoen, set on a sloping hill just above the river. Arranged along a quaint pathway punctuated with pavilions housing a gift shop, seating areas, an outdoor kitchen and a breakfast room, each gracefully proportioned cottage provides private, farm-like living space. Each is charmingly detailed with natural grained wood ceilings and furniture, white plastered walls and sliding papered *shoji* screens reminiscent of an earlier era. The delicate scent of fresh rush *tatami* mats, on which fluffy *futon* are laid out each night, fills the air. Fresh flower arrangements brighten the rooms. Eight of the ten cottages have their own rough-hewn outdoor bathtubs on their verandahs, with forest and river views. These private tubs are complemented by four segregated indoor communal baths and two family baths. Organic farm-fresh meals—a work of art in themselves—are served in the cottages in the evenings by one or more *kimono*-clad women. Breakfast is taken in the specially assigned room overlooking the river. Picnic lunches are available. At the nearby Tenkuh-no-Mori, each of the five villas (two available for rent during the day only, the others for overnight stays) has its own open-air hot spring bath. Most striking are the wooden verandahs outside each villa, wonderful locales from which to practice yoga or simply take in the scenery.

The Tajimas' love of the land and their craftsmanship in providing the luxuries of silence, homegrown organic cooking and mineral-rich bathing on a mountaintop make their retreats a highly memorable experience.

Above: The stunning open-air hot spring bath built into the deck at Hanachiru Sato Villa.
Opposite top: The bedroom at Tenkuh Villa is detailed with rich natural woods.
Left: Organic vegetables are grown on-site.
Right: The tranquil Akanesasu Oka Villa, one of the three available for overnight stays at Tenkuh-no-Mori.

Address: Gajoen
4230 Shukukubota, Makizono-cho, Kirishima-shi,
Kagoshima-ken 899-6507, Japan
Tel: +81 995 77 2114; **Fax:** +81 995 77 2203
Website: www.gajoen.jp
Address: Tenkuh-no-Mori
3389 Shukukubota, Makizono-cho, Kirishima-shi
Kagoshima-ken 899-6507, Japan
Tel: +81 995 76 0777; **Fax:** +81 995 76 0778
E-mail: tenkuh@po.minc.ne.jp

Above: The elegant reception area at
Gosho Bessho.
Opposite: A communal hot spring bath
filled with "gold spring" waters.

Gosho Bessho Kobe

Located on the northern slopes of Mount Rokko within the Kansai district of Kobe, Hyogo Prefecture–the cities of Kobe and Osaka lie on the mountain's southern side–Arima Onsen is one of the largest hot spring resorts in Japan. It is also one of the oldest, with a history of over a thousand years, and a very good destination for a first introduction to a hot spring resort. The town's recorded history goes back to the seventh-century *Nihon Shoki*. The town center, which can easily be explored on foot, consists of a maze of narrow streets lined with traditional houses with white *kura* (storehouses), Japanese-style *onsen ryokan* (spa inns), historic Buddhist temples and Shinto shrines, souvenir shops selling the famous Arima straw ware curios, and sundry shops selling the equally famous Tansan-Senbei cripsy crackers made from carbonated hot spring water.

The waters at Arima Onsen are of two types. "Gold springs" (*Kinsen*) are yellow-brown in color thanks to their iron and salt content, while "silver springs" (*Ginsen*) are colorless and, it is said, mildly radioactive. Although water gushes up freely from springs, most visitors opt to soak in the steaming waters at public bathhouses or at the *ryokan* open to day-trippers. Footbaths set along local roads allow locals as well as tourists to soak their feet while literally soaking in the atmosphere of the quaint town.

Left: Elegantly presented French cuisine is available at the resort.
Right: Wooden floors and Western furniture replace rush *tatami* mats in the spacious Thermal Suite, but the overall ambience remains Japanese.

Address: Gosho Bessho
958 Arima-cho, Kita-ku
Kobe 651-1401, Hyogo-ken, Japan
Tel: +78 904 0554
Fax: +78 904 3601
E-mail: goshobessho@goshobo.co.jp
Website: www.goshobo.co.jp/
goshobessho/

Left: A classic Japanese garden faces the low-key entrance porch.
Right: A thermal room with hot tub is attached to all guest rooms at Gosho Bessho.
Below: A valley view from the upstairs balcony of a guest room.

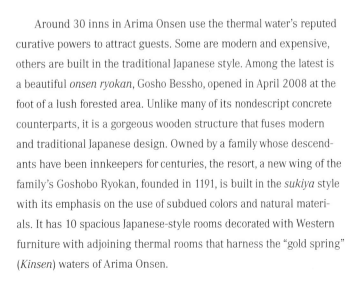

Around 30 inns in Arima Onsen use the thermal water's reputed curative powers to attract guests. Some are modern and expensive, others are built in the traditional Japanese style. Among the latest is a beautiful *onsen ryokan*, Gosho Bessho, opened in April 2008 at the foot of a lush forested area. Unlike many of its nondescript concrete counterparts, it is a gorgeous wooden structure that fuses modern and traditional Japanese design. Owned by a family whose descendants have been innkeepers for centuries, the resort, a new wing of the family's Goshobo Ryokan, founded in 1191, is built in the *sukiya* style with its emphasis on the use of subdued colors and natural materials. It has 10 spacious Japanese-style rooms decorated with Western furniture with adjoining thermal rooms that harness the "gold spring" (*Kinsen*) waters of Arima Onsen.

Inn Seiryuso Shimoda

An enormous stone lantern at the flagstone-staired, willow-lined entrance and a vast 82-foot (25-meter) thermal swimming pool distinguish Seiryuso from other spa inns at the historically significant port town of Shimoda on the Izu Peninsula, a two-and-a-half hour ride by fast train from Tokyo or a 30-minute hop by helicopter from Tokyo's Narita Airport to the resort's helipad. Sitting in quiet serenity on the banks of the Inouzawa River amidst 10 acres (4 hectares) of typical Japanese landscaped gardens, Seiryuso, which dates back to the Edo period (1603–1868), embodies the very essence of Japanese accommodation, be it in the way of architecture, lifestyle, nature, traditions or culture. The inn is generously endowed with clear running streams and hot water springs that feed its outside and inside baths. The natural spring waters not only flow into the spa inn at temperatures of over 100 degrees Fahrenheit (38 degrees Centigrade)–which are then lowered to a more comfortable 88 degrees Fahrenheit

Left: A guest relaxing in the wood-heated Finnish-style sauna.

Below: The "garden" spa facilities include the swimming pool and surrounding baths and treatment rooms.

Right: Another view of the communal outdoor thermal pool Rinken.

(31 degrees Centigrade)–but are so abundant (they flow at an impressive (550 liters) per minute) they can fully renew the mild alkaline water in the swimming pool twice daily.

Innkeeper Hideo Tanaka has consciously combined the traditional Japanese *onsen ryokan* (spa inn) with elements of ancient Roman baths, promoting the resort not only as a place to improve health but also for discussion of philosophy or art. Amidst the silence and steam, visitors can stretch and glide by day through the spa swimming pool or soak by moonlight in the sheltered open thermal pool while contemplatively regarding the resort's 100-year-old willows, swaying bamboos, regal palms, meticulously clipped bushes and lovely stone lanterns. The gently sloping forests of the surrounding Amagi Mountains, which change their colors with the seasons, add to the tranquil environment.

Many of Seiryuso's 26 rooms, built along the Japanese concept of *ma* or space, with large, unfussy, almost empty rooms and *en suite* facilities, have garden or spa pool views. Twenty-four rooms have private indoor spa baths. Three communal hot water baths, a steam room, a wood-heated Finnish-style sauna, treatments with natural oils and body rubs with special clay are all designed to overcome body aches, hypertension and other ailments. The productive sea and soil of the Izu Peninsula allows guests to dine in style on a variety of high-grade fish, game and seasonal garden produce.

Address: Seiryuso
2-2 Kochi, Shimoda-shi
Shizuoka-ken 415-0011
Japan
Tel: +81 558 22 1361
Fax: +81 558 23 2066
E-mail: info@seiryuso.co.jp
Website: www.seiryuso.co.jp

Left: Tubs and wooden chairs.
Right: The guest rooms embody the very essence of traditional Japanese accommodation.
Pages 86–87: The 82-foot (25-meter) swimming pool at the heart of the resort is fed with water from the hot springs.

Thalassa Shima Hotel & Resort

Opened in August 1992, the Thalassa Shima Hotel & Resort, a four-hour journey by train from Tokyo, combines the facilities of a luxury hotel with a unique and increasingly popular therapy originating in France. Thalasso therapy uses seawater, seaweed and sea mud treatments to combat stress, fatigue and excess weight. The Thalassa Shima Resort Hotel is located on Shirahama Beach facing Toba Bay on the Kii Peninsula along the southeast coast of Mie Prefecture. Touting the theme "Body and soul relaxation," it is the first hotel in Asia to offer authentic Thalasso therapy, the second being the Ayana Resort & Spa in Bali (page 28). The freshness of the seawater and the serene, unpolluted environment along the coast are deemed highly suitable for this special therapy. The seawater is piped from some 790 yards (720 meters) offshore at a depth of 40 feet (12 meters). Each client is said to use 1.5 tons of seawater per day in the treatment. Little surprise then that people who undergo the therapy are revitalized in both spirit and mind.

Complementing the Thalassa therapy treatments are four other aesthetic beauty treatments, supported by facilities such as a heated indoor swimming pool, fitness center, sauna and outdoor Jacuzzi. The hotel's French restaurant, Lumiere, also offers a special light menu of natural, healthy foods based on the LOHAS

Above: The Royal Suite offers soothing views.

Right: Madam Katoko Konno, a world-famous facial aesthetician.

Bottom: Algotherapic treatment using seaweed.

Opposite top: The heated seawater Jacuzzi on the terrace.

Opposite middle: Freshly squeezed healthy juices.

Opposite bottom: All guest rooms overlook the ocean.

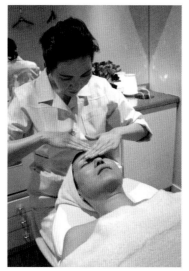

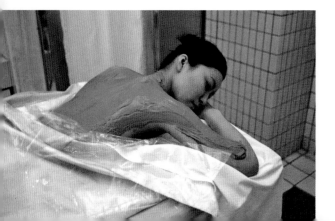

Address: Thalassa Shima Hotel & Resort
1826-1 Shirahama, Uramura-cho
Toba City, Mie-ken
Japan 517-0025
Tel: +81 599 32 1111
Fax: +81 599 32 1109
E-mail: reservation@thalasso.co.jp
Website: www.thalasso.co.jp

(Lifestyles of Health and Sustainability) concept. The hotel's dietitian is on hand for individual consultation on nutrition and diets to be followed during a guest's stay and later on at home. The modern, elegant Thalassa Shima Hotel & Resort has a soothing, subdued atmosphere fitting for a resort dedicated to healing.

When not partaking of the special treatments on offer, guests can enjoy visits to nearby Mikimoto Pearl Island–Toba's main claim to fame is as the birthplace of the cultured pearl industry–and the Toba Aquarium as well as Japan's most sacred shrine, the fifth-century Ise Shrine.

Maison Souvannaphoum

Luang Prabang, the royal capital of Laos for 600 years, until 1975, and a UNESCO World Heritage Site since 1995, is a charming town on the banks of the Mekong River, famous for its glittering temples, spiritual and religious sites and the limestone formations of nearby Kuang Si. The restored Maison Souvannaphoum, once the residence of Prince Souvannaphoum and a mere 10 minutes from the airport, is the perfect base from which to soak up the old-world charm of the town and its environs. Combining colonial-style luxury with contemporary style and modern facilities, the distinctive French provincial-influenced brick structure contains 24 rooms and suites. La Residence wing offers three luxurious suites, named Maison, Laos and Champa, located in the former home of the prince, while the garden and verandah rooms in the Garden Wing are notable for their large balconies from which guests can enjoy sweeping views of the mountains and Mekong, which is within walking distance, and the pool and serene gardens. All rooms at this delightful boutique hotel are decorated with touches of the signature color tangerine.

The Angsana Spa offers rejuvenating treatments using fresh botanical ingredients, as well as Ayurvedic massage and aromatherapy, in three elegant outdoor spa pavilions. For a taste of local food, the Elephant Blanc (white elephant) restaurant serves a variety of mouth-watering French, Laotian and Indochinese dishes in a casual setting by the pool or in the privacy of guests' rooms.

Left: The balconies outside guest rooms are wonderful settings for taking tea and for soaking up the atmosphere of this old royal residence.
Below: Tangerine tones brighten the poolside.

Above: Open-air pavilions at the Angsana Spa.

Left: Colonial charm at the entrance lobby.

Below: Palms in planters add green to the corridor leading to the guest rooms in the Garden Wing.

Right: A contemporary touch in one of the guest rooms – the ubiquitous lotus.

Left: The sparkling blue-tiled pool dominates the garden.
Below: A display of local artifacts and saga tree seeds at the spa.
Bottom: Guest rooms are contemporary in style, with Asian touches.

Address: Maison Souvannaphoum Hotel
Rue Chao Fa Ngum, Banthatluang
Luang Prabang, Laos
Tel: +856 7125 4609
Fax: +856 7121 2577
E-mail: maison@angsana.com

Above: The nine *dhoni* loft suites arrayed along a crescent-shaped walkway, their back decks and steps facing the crystalline lagoon.
Opposite: Decorative palm fruits.

Cocoa Island Maldives

Cocoa Island, a svelte and discrete hideaway in the Maldives, a 40-minute speedboat transfer south of Malé International Airport, is all about cocooning guests, buffering them from the outside world. It is also all about living close to the water's edge, with even its architecture creatively reflecting its island setting. The slender 1,150-foot (350-meter)-long island, known locally as Makunufushi, extends to a sandy spit that temporarily disappears at high tide, and is bordered on all sides by perfect white sand beaches and azure blue waters. Offshore is the Guraidhoo Channel that comes alive each evening with hundreds of dolphins.

Once the property of photographer Eric Klemm, who built a four-bungalow hotel there in 1980, by 2003 Cocoa Island had transformed into the Como Shambhala's *piece de resistance*, an ultra tasteful yet surprisingly simple resort that feels wonderfully spacious yet intensely private. The resort's 36 rooms and suites are a perfect juxtaposition of traditional Maldivian style with modern comforts. Generously spaced along a crescent-shaped wooden walkway built out into the lagoon, magical when lit up at night, the accommodations echo the shape of local *dhoni* fishing boats, with thatched roofs, dark wooden hulls, upturned prows in blue, black and white, porthole windows, and bulbous back sundecks with steps leading down into crystalline waters and the smooth, sandy bed of the lagoon where fish swim undeterred by human interaction.

Address: Makunufushi Island
South Malé Atoll, Republic of Maldives
Tel: +960 441 818
Fax: +960 441 919
E-mail: sales@cocoaisland.como.bz
Website: www.cocoaisland.como.bz

Left: The front of the over-water *dhoni* loft suites, with their distinctive upturned prows and thatched roofs, face the island and swimming pool.
Opposite bottom left: One of the open-sided pavilions at the spa.
Below: Semi-transparent white embroidered drapes temper sunlight in the spacious, clean interiors.
Right: The boat-shaped milky blue concrete and pebble-lined swimming pool seemingly merges with the sea. Landscaping at the resort is minimal.
Right bottom: Permanent footprints in the powdery white sand.

The spacious interiors display contemporary understated luxury at its best: dark wood furniture, pristine white walls, flowing drapes and bright dhurries.

Public facilities are built on the island itself, including the Shambhala Retreat, a series of open pavilions housing spa facilities peppered throughout the frangipani trees, a concrete and pebble-lined infinity-edge swimming pool in the shape of a boat, an open-sided bar with a soaring roof, and a slightly elevated open-plan restaurant with a menu of Indian dishes, Sri Lankan specialties, healthy spa cuisine and fresh seafood. Water-based activities include diving, fishing and sailing.

Kanuhura Maldives

Famed for its laid-back luxury and authentic Maldivian charm, Kanu-hara (formerly part of the One & Only stable but now managed by Sun Resorts) is tucked away on a 3,280-foot (1,000-meter)-long white sand island within the shallow waters of a turquoise lagoon on the eastern rim of Lhaviyani Atoll, a scenic 40-minute seaplane flight north of Malé International Airport. It has two beautiful little island neighbors.

Accommodation is in villas either on the island's coral-sand fringe or in a little village on stilts strung out at the end of a wooden pier in the lagoon with staircases leading directly down to the water. All villas offer views out to the Indian Ocean. The villas are an artful blend of natural materials and contemporary convenience, with spacious, tastefully appointed bedrooms, indoor and outdoor bathrooms and every modern convenience.

The resort's large and shallow lagoon is a prime spot for water sports such as sailing, windsurfing, waterskiing and water scootering. Diving enthusiasts have a mind-boggling choice of more than 40 remote and undisturbed world-class dive sites. Alternatively, guests may choose to chill out by the enormous swimming pool, almost a lagoon in itself, or venture further out on a sunset fishing trip or a dolphin safari. Or rejuvenate at the tranquil spa, one of the largest Asian-style spas in the Maldives, set in its own lavish pavilion and offering a wide menu of treatments. Kanuhara also provides an exceptional and diverse cuisine at the Thin Rah, Olive Tree and Veli Café. In-villa dining is a specialty. The resort's sociable atmosphere is another reason to visit.

Far left: A seaplane or "air taxi" drops guests off at the end of a 660-foot (200 meter)-long jetty.
Left: A yoga lesson in the gym.
Below: The uninhabited island of Jebunuhura reached by a *dhoni* ride from Kanuhura.
Right: A riot of tropical colors in the beach villas, which dot the island's coral sand fringe.
Right bottom: A tub for two with wine and candles.

Address: Kanuhura
Lhaviyani Atoll
Republic of Maldives
Tel: +960 662 0044
Fax: +960 662 0033
E-mail: info@kanuhura.com.mv
Website: www.kanuhura.com

One & Only Reethi Rah Maldives

Among the most ambitious resort developments in the Maldives' 200 inhabited islands (a further 900 are uninhabited) is undoubtedly One & Only Reethi Rah, an artificial paradise with endless white sand coves and turquoise bays opened in May 2005. From a small strip of land in the east side of the North Malé Atoll, about 22 miles (35 km) from Malé International Airport and an hour by speedboat, the island was dramatically enlarged, reclaimed from the shallow lagoon with thousands of tons of sand, to form 12 hand-carved beaches and some 4 miles (6 km) of coastline. From the air, its shape resembles an octopus. The new dimensions guaranteed enough secluded beaches for guests in the 130 villas discretely tucked away from view amidst beautiful landscaping on the island or elevated on stilts over their own patch of ocean.

Privacy, luxury and space are the hallmarks of the resort's villas. Covering a minimum area of 1,450 square feet (135 square meters), they are among the largest resort accommodations in the world, veritable palaces unto themselves. Exquisitely designed in a sophisticated Japanese-meets-Balinese style, all have high, airy ceilings and generous exterior space, ranging from private verandahs and stretches of beach to private swimming pools with large decks. Each has a large stone soaking tub designed for two, an oversized double bathroom and other modern

Top: Reethi Rah, which means "Beautiful Island" in Dhivehi, the local language, occupies one of the largest islands—much of it manmade—in the Maldives.
Right and bottom: The One & Only luxury yacht, modeled on the *dhoni* used by Maldivian fishermen, and its cheery crew.
Opposite: Large net hammocks cantilevered from the decks of the water villas are marvellous for over-water lazing.

comforts. The look of the interiors is sleek and elegantly tropical. Beautiful natural materials are married with contemporary styling.

Gastronomic delights await guests in the resort's three restaurants. Reethi Restaurant fuses flavors from the Far East, Middle East and Mediterranean in its light, contemporary cuisine; the over-the-water Tapasake serves authentic Japanese dishes cooked on the spot; while beachside Fanditha on the northern tip of the island is the place to go for grilled food and salads.

Left: The soaring reception area, its pillars carved with Maldivian floral motifs.

Above: At Tapasake, the over-water restaurant, Japanese dishes are prepared on the spot.

Below: Bathrooms occupy about a third of the space in the water villas and include huge sunken baths by windows and separate shower rooms.

Right: Natural materials and contemporary styling are hallmarks of the wonderfully spacious and airy water villas, perched on stilts in the lagoon. Steps lead down from the front decks to the ocean.

One & Only Reethi Rah also offers a host of activities on and offshore, including tennis, beach football and volleyball, table tennis and indoor games. Guests can also choose from numerous excursions—deep-sea fishing, sunset *dhoni* fishing, dolphin watching, deluxe "desert island" picnics and cultural visits to local islands—in addition to the usual water sports. There is also the fabulous spa, managed by ESPA, which is set in lush gardens and features exotic stress relief therapies ranging from aromatherapy to Indian Ayurveda.

Address: One & Only Reethi Rah
North Malé Atoll, Republic of Maldives
Tel: +960 644 8800
Fax: +960 644 8822
E-mail: info@one&onlyreethirah.com
Website: www.one&onlyreethirah.com

The Rania Experience Maldives

In the Maldivian language of Dhivehi, the name "Rania" derives from the word "Rani," meaning "Queen," and the *Rania*, a luxurious 86-foot (26-meter) Gulf Craft Majesty Yacht is truly worthy of the name. So too is the tiny gem of an island, Maafushi ("small natural island"), and its spa, situated in the middle of one of the largest lagoons in Faafu Atoll, 76 miles (122 km) southwest of Malé International Airport, that are part and parcel of the Rania & Water Garden Island Spa. Opened in 2006 as the ultimate (and most expensive) private island sea escape in the world, the award-winning and bespoke resort, otherwise known as "The Rania Experience," offers guests—limited to one private group of no more than 12–15 at any one time—the freedom to explore the Maldives via a fully crewed, exclusive-use pleasure yacht, then retreat to the seclusion of their own private island.

Left: Sunset over Maafushi.
Above: The skilled hands of a therapist add to the bliss of sun, white talc sand and azure blue sea.
Above right: A tastefully appointed verandah at the three-bedroom Rania Suite.
Right: The island is a haven of natural beauty and tranquility.

On board the *Rania,* guests are accommodated in two handsomely appointed double rooms and two twin rooms. On land, they have full reign of the pristine 7-acre (3-hectare) island, with its palm-fringed powdery white sand beaches and idyllic teal blue lagoon, where the three-bedroom Rania Suite, three adjoining beachfront villas, spa, pool, bar and entertainment lounge provide everything guests need. The yacht and the island villas are stocked with every amenity to meet the exacting tastes of the resort's well-heeled clients, who also enjoy the dedicated services of a private chef, master dive instructor, spa therapist, personal butler and crew. Where and when guests choose to dine or enjoy a tempting menu of Thai and Ayurvedic spa treatments is entirely up to them. Big game fishing, night fishing, sunset, sunrise and moonlight cruises, local island visits and snorkeling add to the allure of "The Rania Experience" and live up to its tagline: "One island, One Yacht, One million possibilities."

Address: The Rania Experience
Faafu Atoll, Republic of Maldives
Tel: +960 674 0555
Fax: +960 674 0557
E-mail: info@raniaexperience.com
Website: www.raniaexperience.com

Above: Plantation shutters add colonial charm and nostalgia.

Right: The Information Centre of Malaysia's most famous tea brand, Boh (Best of Highlands), offers spectacular views of its rolling tea plantation.

Cameron Highlands Resort

At 5,000 feet (1,500 meters) above sea level, the Cameron Highlands are the highest part of Peninsular Malaysia, with a climate rather like a cool English summer. Discovered by British surveyor William Cameron on a mapping expedition in 1885, the highlands became a popular "hill station" for British expatriates during the colonial era as a place to relax and escape the lowland tropical heat and where they could re-create a British lifestyle of English cottages, rose gardens, narrow village lanes, invigorating walks and rounds of golf. British planters also soon realized the potential of the fertile mountain slopes for growing tea, then a prized commodity, and visitors today can still enjoy magnificent views over the rolling tea plantations and see the workers harvesting the leaves by hand.

The mock Tudor architecture of the tranquil boutique Cameron Highlands Resort, set on a lush hillock with vast views over the golf course and the misty hills beyond, continues the colonial feel, as does the hotel's interior, which resembles a genteel English colonial home. Welcoming fireplaces, plush settees and armchairs in the Reading

Left and opposite far right and bottom: Typical English afternoon teas of home-baked scones, finger sandwiches, light-as-air pastries and fresh strawberries and cream, accompanied by Cameron Highlands tea, are a ritual in the elegant and relaxing Jim Thompson Tea Room. **Right:** White walls, lots of dark wood and four-poster beds define the deluxe suites.

Address: Cameron Highlands Resort
39000 Tanah Rata, Cameron Highlands,
Pahang Darul Makmur
Malaysia
Tel: +603 2783 1000
Fax: +603 2148 7397
E-mail: travelcentre@ytlhotels.com.my
Website: www.cameronhighlandsresort.com

Room and Highlands Bar and four-poster beds, polished floors, beamed ceilings and plantation shutters in the 56 rooms embody the charm and gentility of the colonial lifestyle.

In keeping with its tagline "Trails, Tales and Tradition," the resort capitalizes not only on its scenery and old English charm but also on the mysterious disappearance of famous American businessman and "Thai silk king" Jim Thompson during a holiday in the highlands in 1967. His name comes alive in the resort's Jim Thompson Tea Room where guests can enjoy the time-honored tradition of English afternoon tea with homemade scones topped with fresh cream and Cameron strawberries, washed down with a selection of Cameron Highland teas, and ruminate on the theories surrounding Thompson's disappearance.

The resort also has an impressive spa where the tea theme is continued with signature tea baths and other therapies and massages inspired by the restorative properties of tea.

Left: Carcosa's entrance hall with stairs leading up to the suites.
Right: A front view of the eclectic half-timbered Carcosa Seri Negara. The large open terrace above the entrance is part of the hotel's master suite.
Bottom: A wicker chair and an English afternoon tea on the verandah.

Carcosa Seri Negara Kuala Lumpur

Regally perched atop a hill and set in 4 acres (1.6 hectares) of lush gardens within the beautiful Lake Gardens, minutes from the hurly-burly of downtown Kuala Lumpur, is a legacy from Malaysia's colonial past. Comprising two identical, carefully restored paper-white mansions—Carcosa, once the official residence of the British governor of Malaya, and Seri Negara, used at the time to accommodate distinguished guests visiting the colonial state—this reinvented luxury boutique hotel is a perfect combination of aesthetics and function.

The public areas of the imposing hotel, dotted with Malaysian antiques and *objets d'art*, remain bastions of bygone Britishness. English high tea served in the elegant drawing room or on the charming wraparound verandah overlooking the manicured grounds, candle-lit meals in the dining room followed by cigars on the verandah, and Sunday curry tiffins are reminders of the colonial past. The classic décor of the bar is reminiscent of pre-war British pubs.

The hotel's 13 Victorian-style plush and palatial suites, named after the 13 states of Malaysia, are the epitome of timeless elegance. Each is individually decorated. Some boast separate living rooms with garden views, others generous balconies and private dining rooms. All have spacious bedrooms and bathrooms. Despite their classic look, the suites are fully

Left: Chocolate and cream-colored tiles and green palms in pots on the breezy verandah.
Right and below: The spacious bedrooms are furnished in a quintessentially English style.
Bottom: The broad wraparound verandah, with its comfortable wicker furniture, is the perfect spot for tea, a good book or simply gazing at the gardens.

equipped with all the modern conveniences required by travelers. Butlers provide personalized, round-the-clock service.

Carcosa Seri Negara is the ideal retreat for those wishing to relive the pleasures of the past while enjoying the modern conveniences of a city very much immersed in the present, whose skyscrapers can be glimpsed through the tropical trees and shrubs surrounding this resolutely colonial oasis.

Address: Carcosa Seri Negara
Taman Tasik Perdana
50480 Kuala Lumpur
Malaysia
Tel: +603 2295 0888
Fax: +603 2282 7888
E-mail: carcosa@ghmhotels.com
Website: www.ghmhotels.com

Left: An old Malay-style pavilion set within a tranquil coconut palm-fringed pond.
Right: The superb beach offers stunning views out to an islet-dotted emerald ocean.

Four Seasons Resort Langkawi

Built on the site of a former coconut plantation on the northern edge of the largest of the 99 islands forming the Langkawi archipelago off the west coast of Malaysia, the Four Seasons is a heady combination of Third World unde-veloped natural beauty and First World amenities. Behind, towering over the resort, are limestone cliffs and rainforest. In front, facing the Andaman Sea is the picturesque beach of Tanjung Rhu, a gorgeous strip of white sand and a premier spot for viewing the sensational sunsets that burst into life beyond the craggy limestone islets dotting the sea.

Covering an area of 48 acres (19.4 heactares), the resort has the feel of a traditional Malay village but blends intricate decorative details from other Asian as well as Moorish cultures. The grand entrance passes through imposing temple-style laterite walls from Thailand; the domed reception area, dramatic courtyards and sun-bathed bathrooms are reminiscent of an Arabian sultan's palace; and Spanish marble, gray slate and burnished steel, inspired by Granada's Alhambra, showcase Islamic art and culture. The resort is large, comprising a series of central pavilions and pools scattered within lushly landscaped grounds. All 91 rooms, including 68 two-story pavilions (of four units each) and 20 one-unit bedroom villas, are oriented toward the sea, and are decorated in muted, nature-inspired colors. The most exclusive are tweaked with such luxurious touches as private spa rooms and plunge pools.

Other highlights of the resort include an infinity pool with cabanas framed by stone walls for privacy, and a beautifully embellished royal tent from Rajasthan, India, the scene for romantic dining on the beach.

Left: A view from the fish-scale tiled roofed Ikan-Ikan restaurant, which specializes in fish and other local dishes.

Below: The approach to the beachfront villas.

Right: The one-bedroom beachfront villas include a private pool garden, patio, spa treatment room and huge lounge.

Opposite bottom left: The main swimming pool is a fantasy of sea-related sculptures.

Opposite bottom right: Moorish elements are visible in the metalwork, be it a latticed arch or a hanging lamp.

Address: Four Seasons Resort Langkawi
Jalan Tanjung Rhu
07000 Langkawi Island
Kedah Darul Aman, Malaysia
Tel: +604 950 8888
Fax: +604 950 8899
E-mail: reservations.lan@fourseasons.com
Website: www.fourseasons.com/langkawi

Above and opposite top left: At the luxurious spa, where pavilions appear to float amongst reflecting ponds, treatments are borrowed from Bali and India.
Opposite top right: Malaysian and Moorish influences abound in the architecture and fittings of the expansive bedrooms.
Right: A corner of the reception area has a Middle Eastern atmosphere.

Above: Water and forest at the resort's Spa Village.
Right: Villas on stilts in the ocean and lush rainforest viewed from the Spa Village's long, narrow infinity-edge lap pool, which drops down to a narrow beach.

Pangkor Laut Resort

"How beautiful God has made this paradise!" the late, great tenor Luciano Pavarotti reportedly exclaimed when he helped open privately owned Panglor Laut Island with a concert in 1994 (he returned with a full orchestra in 2000). Located 3 miles (5 km) off the west coast of Malaysia's Perak state, about four hours by road from the capital, Kuala Lumpur, and a further 45 minutes by boat, 80 percent of the island's 300 acres (122 hectares) are cloaked in dense tropical rainforest and under the philosophy of "one island, one resort" will remain so. The island is home to an astonishing biodiversity, perhaps the most remarkable being the great pied hornbills that take flight from casuarinas and palms and soar over the island.

Built in stages over a couple of decades (it started life as the Pansy Resort in 1985), Pangkor Laut has been progressively expanded and refurbished. It now comprises three distinct areas. The original resort, built around Royal Bay, is a collection of Malay-style villas perched atop stilts connected by wooden boardwalks over the sea (the first Malaysian resort to feature this type of accommodation), with some garden and hillside villas clustered around public facilities housed in pavilions, and a lovely lap pool fronting the ocean and jetty. The second area, on the other side of the island, comprises an exclusive collection of nine magnificent purpose-built and beautifully landscaped complexes, called Estates, four fronting the beach and five on a ridge within the rainforest. From film stars to financiers, this is where the well-heeled head for a minimum three-night stay complete with personal butler and chef. The third

area, at Coral Bay, and the most recent (it was opened in 2000), is the elegant Spa Village on the south coast of the island, a village-sized complex of 22 over-water villas, treatment pavilions, bath houses, semi-private "nap" gazebos and a 164-foot (50-meter) lap pool with an infinity edge. All face the sea and are interspersed with open courtyards, lotus ponds, an herb garden and a reflexology path.

In addition to this three-in-one concept, Pangkor Laut has its own resort beach, Emerald Bay, reached by a short hike across the island's spine. The horse-shoe shaped cove, cupped between long, rainforest-clad headlands, with huge indigenous gnarled trees (not the usual coconut palms) descending to the end of the perfect yellow sand beach, and its translucent emerald green waters is Pangkor Laut's true gem; it is entirely undisturbed by any permement buildings.

The inactive can simply enjoy the beach, pools, spa and views, but for the active there are various options, including fishing, mildly intrepid jungle trekking (a resident naturalist is on hand), a cruise-cum-snorkeling trip on one of the resort's oriental teak junks to a sheltered cove for a lunchtime barbecue or sunset dinner, or a round of golf at the nearby links. Dining at the resort's six restaurants serving authentic Malay and traditional Chinese cuisine is an experience in itself. Three of the restaurants are attractively perched on the edge of the sea.

Address: Pangkor Laut Resort
32200 Lumut
Perak, Malaysia
Tel: +605 699 1100
Fax: +605 699 1200
E-mail: plr@ytlhotels.com.my
Website: www.pangkorlautresort.com

The Datai Langkawi

Tucked away on an elevated site in the middle of rainforest overlooking beautiful Datai Bay on the northwestern tip of Langkawi Island, the largest of the 99 islands forming the Langkawi archipelago off the west coast of Malaysia, the Datai is the last word in hideaway luxury. Built in warm local woods and natural stone that blend harmoniously with its lush, green surroundings, the resort, which bills itself as a "Retreat to Nature," appears to emerge from the rainforest floor before meandering down the hill to the sea where a seductive and private white sand beach awaits guests. The sounds of the rainforest permeate, from the soporific buzz of a million cicadas to the honks of hornbills and the calls of other tropical birds to the chatter of long-tailed macaque monkeys. Sea eagles and brahminy kites patrol the skies. The resort has just the right combination of wildness and civilization. It is a peaceful place, a tranquil antidote to the urban hum, perfect for honeymooners in search of seclusion or the jaded in need of respite.

The hotel has just 112 deluxe rooms, suites and villas (some on stilts over water). Barely visible from the sea, the main complex—84 rooms and suites housed around the central lobby and main swimming pool—is hidden by forest on a high ridge, yet offers fantastic

Above: The stunning two-story Pavilion restaurant overlooks the swimming pool.

Right, below and opposite top: The superior rooms, housed around the central lobby, make use of local wood and have cantilevered balconies offering fantastic vistas.

Opposite bottom: The main swimming pool, a prism of perfection engulfed within a canopy of tropical greenery, is a tranquil back-to-nature antidote to the urban hum.

Address: The Datai
Jalan Teluk Datai
07000 Langkawi Island
Kedah Darul Aman, Malaysia
Tel: +604 959 2500
Fax: +604 959 2600
E-mail: datai@ghmhotels.com
Website: www.ghmhotels.com

vistas over the tropical canopy to the sea beyond. Smaller Malay-style villas stud the hillside below the main complex, nestled within the forest canopy and linked by covered walkways, paths, bridges and steps. Rivaling the imposing lobby, an expansive open-beamed structure with massive shingled roof, is the awe-inspiring tree house-style restaurant, aptly called The Pavilion, which is perched atop 45-foot (14-meter)-high unplaned tree trunks that jut out from the ridge.

The luxury spa, set in rain forest to one side of the hotel, offers not just a plethora of scrubs, wraps, facials, massages and full body services, but also conducts spa workshops where guests can learn how to massage their partners and how to mix the ingredients to make their favorite scrub.

The Magellan Sutera

Located on 384 acres (155 hectares) of prime reclaimed seafront, with the majestic Mount Kinabalu as its backdrop, the Magellan Sutera is part of Asia's first fully integrated and complete lifestyle resort that also includes the Pacific Sutera, Sutera Harbour Marina, Golf and Country Club, and The Residences at Sutera Harbour. That such a large resort should be built in Kota Kinabalu, the gateway to Sabah, Malaysia's largest island state to the east of the Peninsula, is no surprise. Sabah is not only home to some of the world's most extraordinary species of plants and animals, but its magnificent mountain is a challenge for climbers and its underwater treasures a treat for divers. Adventure sports, cultural experiences and a melting pot of 32 diverse ethnic groups combine to make Sabah one of the most interesting and popular destinations in Asia.

The Magellan Sutera, named after Ferdinand Magellan, captain of the first maritime expedition to circumnavigate the world, is an ideal base from which to explore Kota Kinabalu and its hinterland. The hotel's 436 rooms and suites are accommodated in a series of buildings inspired by the multistory longhouses of the Rungus people and are clustered around a grand longhouse-style lobby. Ethnic Sabah design is tastefully incorporated into the décor of the rooms and public spaces. Private balconies offer views over the hotel's beautifully landscaped gardens or the island-dotted South China Sea.

Address: The Magellan Sutera
1 Sutera Harbour Boulevard
88100 Kota Kinabalu, Sabah
Malaysia
Tel: +6088 303 900
Fax: +6088 317 540
E-mail: sutera@suteraharbour.
com.my
Website: MagellanSutera-
KotaKinabalu.com

Back from the rigors of jungle trekking, mountain climbing or diving, a round of golf on the hotel's beautiful 27-hole Magellan golf course, or an energetic swim in one of the many pools, guests can pamper themselves with a superb choice of rejuvenating massages, body scrubs and beauty therapies that use natural herbs, flowers and spices in the hotel's spacious two-level Mandara Spa. Signature services comprise warm stone massage, ocean detox and Yin & Yang "him and her" packages.

Choices for dining are many and varied. In line with the preservation of Sabah's floral and fauna, the Endangered Species Café and Swim-Up Bar feature healthy lifestyle food and beverages. Ferdinand's, an elegant Italian restaurant, together with the Five Sails, Spice Islands and Seafood Palace restaurants means diners are spoilt for choice.

Left: The 134-foot (41-meter)-high canopy walkway at Poring Hot Springs in Mount Kinabalu National Park.
Top left: Feeding fish at Manukan Island, the second largest island in the Tunku Abdul Rahman Marine Park, 20 minutes by boat from Kota Kinabalu.
Top right: Bornean pigmy elephants at the city's Lok Kawi Wildlife Park.
Above: *Nepenthes Rajah*, the world's largest pitcher plant, spotted along the Mesilau Nature Trail, one of the routes to the mountain's summit.
Right: Sunset cruise on *Puteri Sutera*.

Right: A view of the open-air hot spring pool from Soyan restaurant.
Below: Soyan restaurant serves healthy French cuisine in a peaceful setting overlooking the Nanshi River.
Opposite: A waterfall at the nearby Neidung Park, one of the main attractions available to visitors.

Spring Park Urai Spa & Resort Taiwan

One of a new generation of hot spring retreats that combine the right raw materials with the European spa concept, Spring Park Urai Spa & Resort in Wulai, a short jaunt from Taipei, has all the ingredients necessary for promoting overall good health: invigorating springs that bubble and flow with hot, healthy mineral water, new health treatments and light and healthy cuisine. The resort, located along the banks of the sparkling blue-green Nanshi River that snakes its way among steep and scenic green hills, shares the most famous sodium bicarbonate hot springs in northern Taiwan with other resorts in the Wulai area. Dubbed "Spring Beauty," the spring waters are colorless and odorless, and although temperatures can reach 185 degrees Fahrenheit (85 degrees Celsius), the waters are kept naturally comfortable by an influx of cool river water. The area is also famous as the home of the Atayal, one of 12 recognized aboriginal peoples in Taiwan, and their influence is seen in the architecture and décor of the resort.

Spring Park Urai, opened in October 2000, is housed in a striking building with a superb view of the river, the outdoor dining area and the open-air hot spring pool. Made of natural materials such as stone and wood and decorated with aboriginal artwork, the building contains 23 stylish guest rooms, some with private thermal pools, and a restaurant serving French cuisine. In keeping

Left: Shades of green—forest, river, pool and plants—and the sounds of water combine to soothe the senses.
Right: Elegant, understated décor in a guest room.
Below left: The riverside terrace, an ideal setting for snacks and light meals.
Below right: A seaweed salad, typical of the resort's emphasis on light, healthy cusine.
Bottom: The streetside view and entrance to the resort.

Address: Spring Park Urai Spa & Resort
No. 3 Yanti Wulai Shiang
Wulai 233
Taipei County
Taiwan
Tel: 1-214-357-5522
Website: www.springpaerhotel.com.tw

with the latest global food trends in hot springs cuisine, the emphasis at the resort's food outlets is on fresh seasonal produce, locally grown fruit and vegetables, native seafood, water-rich organic foods that clean out the bloodsteam, and healthy drinks like mineral water, fruit juices and green tea.

No visit to Wulai is complete without a stroll through the town's main street where gift shops sell Atayal handicrafts, a variety of millet wines and *mochi*, a traditional aboriginal sticky rice dessert in peanut, red bean, taro and other flavors.

Above: Elephants carved on wooden doors.
Right: The bold reception area features a lofty ceiling supported by ornately decorated pillars, a huge screen carved with mythical *naga* serpents, tiered candles in brass holders, and wall panels featuring the resort's hallmark elephant.

Anantara Golden Triangle Chiang Rai

Perched high above the dawn mist on a hill ridge overlooking the confluence of the Ruak and Mekong Rivers where Thailand, Laos and Myanmar meet—the mysterious and alluring Golden Triangle—is the stunningly beautiful Anantara Golden Triangle Resort & Spa, opened in October 2003. Set amidst 160 acres (64 hectares) of indigenous forest and landscaped gardens in Chiang Rai, Thailand's northernmost province, the resort is a magical mix of nature, culture and modern luxury. A multitude of unforgettable experiences await guests: soaking up panoramic views of the jungle canopy to the serpentine Mekong River from the startling hilltop infinity-edge pool; learning to be a mahout (elephant driver) at the resort's unique Elephant Camp, home to rescued elephants from the streets of Thailand's biggest cities as well as the resort's resident elephants; riding an elephant through bamboo jungle along the Burmese border; experiencing the rush of a longboat up the Mekong to Laos; learning the basic techniques of preparing Thai dishes at the Anantara Cooking School; absorbing the vibrant culture of the region with guided visits

Above: Heat treatments at the Anantara Spa employ local herbs and spices.

Below: Teak furniture, Thai silk textiles, Thai artifacts and original paintings make for elegant luxury in the guest rooms. Canopied daybeds are a special feature on the balconies of the 19 signature Anatara Suites.

Right: A suspended daybed in the Anantara Spa.

Opposite top: Sampling the sway of an elephant along a bamboo forest trail.

Opposite bottom: The rectangular main swimming pool.

Address: Anantara Golden Triangle Resort & Spa
229 Mooi, Chiang Saen
Chiang Rai 57150, Thailand
Tel: +66 (0) 5378 4084
Fax: +66 (0) 5378 4090
E-mail: goldentriangle@anantara.com
Website: www.goldentriangle.anantara.com

to local hilltribe villages and excursions to border markets; pampering one's taste buds at the resort's signature restaurants and bars; or rejuvenating with a traditional Thai massage at the king-size Anantara Spa.

The architecture of the resort and its interiors, both public and private, exude a contemporary interpretation of classic Thai design. All 77 rooms and suites feature large balconies, 58 of them with views of all three countries, with built-in sofas and spaces for private dining, and all are decorated with local arts and crafts that reflect the area's distinctive hilltribe and Buddhist cultures.

Baan Taling Ngam Resort Koh Samui

Located on Koh Samui's secluded and tranquil west coast, a 40-minute drive from the island's international airport, the 16-acre (6-hectare) Baan Taling Ngam Resort & Spa (formerly Le Royal Meridien Baan Taling Ngam) is nestled into the side of a cliff surrounded by thousands of gently swaying coconut trees. Cascading down the cliff on three levels, and offering stunning panoramic views of the Gulf of Thailand and the 40 or so islands dotting its turquoise waters that make up the Ang Thong National Marine Park, are the hotel's lobby and restaurants, guest rooms, spa and pools. The resort's signature pool, the first infinity-edge pool to be built on Koh Samui, appears to spill over its edges into the coconut palm grove below.

The beach at the bottom of the cliff, where a second swimming pool is located, is small by resort standards, but is compensated by the wealth of activities available: catamaran sailing, kayaking, snorkeling and windsurfing on the water and tennis and mountain biking on land. A dive school offers courses.

The accommodations at Baan Taling Ngam comprise 70 deluxe rooms and suites as well as two- and three-bedroom private villas. Five of the cliff villas have private plunge pools. All rooms are beautifully decorated in traditional Thai style, with teak furniture, antiques, exquisite textiles and pretty louvered doors leading to the balconies and terraces.

The two-level spa features six luxuriously appointed indoor and outdoor treatments suites, all with breathtaking sea views. The spa is the first in Thailand to use only "Chi" water, with its special detoxifying and re-energizing properties, in its treatments. Signature treatments include the herbal face mask and oatmeal body wash.

Left and above: At the luxurious spa, outside baths and private steam rooms are integrated with indoor and outdoor treatment suites set high above the ocean.
Below: Peaceful beachside living is guaranteed at an oceanfront villa.
Right: A panoramic view of the terraced resort and scenic Andaman Sea.
Right bottom: The reception at the spa is decorated with beautiful red lacquerware.

Address: Baan Taling Ngam Resort & Spa
295 Moo 3, Taling Ngam Beach,
West Coast, Ko Samui
Surat Thani 84140
Thailand
Tel: +66 77 42 9100
Fax: 66 77 42 3220
E-mail: reservations@baan-taling-ngam.com
Website: www.baan-taling-ngam.com

Blue Canyon Country Club Phuket

Blue Canyon Country Club at Mai Khao on Phuket, Thailand's largest island, located some 535 miles (862 km) south of Bangkok, has a reputation as one of the most legendary, exclusive and finest private golf clubs in Asia. Cradled in a secluded 720-acre (290-hectare) valley against a backdrop of the majestic Phang Nga Mountains and the Andaman Sea, and just minutes from Phuket International Airport, the club basks in the island's reputation as the "pearl of the Andaman" or the "pearl of the south" for its tropical sunshine, natural heritage (limestone cliffs, powdery white beaches, broad bays and inland forests), world-renowned diving sites and world-class accommodations.

Blue Canyon comprises two award-winning 18-hole championship golf courses surrounded by freshwater lakes, a 49-bedroom Golfers' Lodge, luxurious resort apartments and villas for sale or lease, and a large and opulent clubhouse with every imaginable facility, including a spa. The golf courses, which were originally molded in 1988 around existing canyons, woodlands, an old tin mine and rubber plantations to ensure minimal disruption to the existing landscape, offer two contrasting layouts. The Lakes Course, as its name implies, has water

Above: A classy Canyon Suite at the 49-bedroom Golfers' Lodge.
Below and opposite top: The spa offers specially developed therapies for golfers.

hazards hampering 17 of its 18 holes. The Canyon Course is contoured into a deep valley with tree-lined fairways and rolling hills. Several golfing greats have played at Blue Canyon Country Club, including Greg Norman and Tiger Woods, and in 1998 the club played host to the Johnnie Walker Classic.

The award-winning spa at Blue Canyon Country Club provides a comprehensive and exotic range of treatments, from stress-reduction to energy-promotion therapies, many specially designed to meet the needs of golfers and guests. The Canyon Restaurant, serving fusion cuisine, and the open-air Golfers' Terrace both have fine views over the Canyon Course.

For a break from golf, visitors to the Blue Canyon Country Club can venture to beautiful Nai Yang Beach, 5 minutes south of the airport, or to Phuket Town, just 18 miles (30 km) away.

Address: Blue Canyon Country Club
165 Moo 1, Thepkasattri Road
Thalang, Phuket 83110
Thailand
Tel: +66 76 328 088
Fax: +66 76 328 068
E-mail: reservation@bluecanyonclub.com
Website: www.bluecanyonclub.com

Right: A plaque in the clubhouse contains the names of luminaries who have set course records at the club, including Fred Couples, Greg Norman and Tiger Woods.
Below: The 9th hole of the Canyon Course, surrounded by obvious natural hazards.

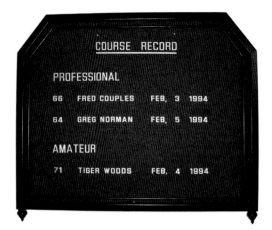

COURSE RECORD

PROFESSIONAL

66   FRED COUPLES   FEB. 3 1994

64   GREG NORMAN   FEB. 5 1994

AMATEUR

71   TIGER WOODS   FEB. 4 1994

Chiva-Som Hua Hin

Chiva-Som, meaning "Haven of Life," is an all-inclusive health resort set on 7 acres (3 hectares) of beachside land at Hua Hin, one of the oldest and most popular resorts on the Gulf of Thailand, 124 miles (200 km) south of Bangkok. Not only are the facilities at Chiva-Som International Health Resort world class but its pioneering combination of traditional Asian therapies with Western health and wellness and its philosophy of rest, relaxation and improvement sets it apart from hotels and resorts with spa or health facilities. This is not just another beach spa getaway. On arrival at the spa, guests meet with a qualified health and wellness consultant to evaluate health basics and tailor a program of treatments and activities to achieve their personal goals. Packages range from 1–3 day stays or 10–28 day retreats.

In the center of Chiva-Som lies a cluster of elegant guest pavilions inspired by traditional Thai architecture, surrounded by lushly landscaped gardens with lakes and waterfalls. At the far end of the grounds, overlooking the Gulf of Thailand, are Western-style guest rooms with king-size beds, plenty of teak and spacious terraces or balconies. With only 57 rooms and suites, and an equal number of indoor and outdoor treatment rooms, together with 80 rigorously trained therapists and world-renowned experts on well-being, Chiva-Som is an exclusive retreat, the very place to examine and change your lifestyle. No expense has been spared to provide a controlled

environment so that actual health benefits can be gained from a stay there. The dedicated health resort offers a wide range of services and a smorgasbord of classes—a mind-boggling 130 in all. Fitness therapy includes pilates, super stretch, sea kayaking, aquatic therapy, power walking, dancing, Thai boxing, tai chi, four types of yoga—the list goes on and on. Likewise, there are 16 different types of massage therapy.

Chiva-Som also places great emphasis on a balanced diet. Its acclaimed spa cuisine of Asian and Western specialties is detoxifying, fat- and salt-free and is as tasty as it is healthy. Many of the ingredients for its detox juices and raw food options are grown in Chiva-Som's own organic gardens.

It is not surprising that guests depart Chiva-Som with a deeper understanding of their own health—and many return.

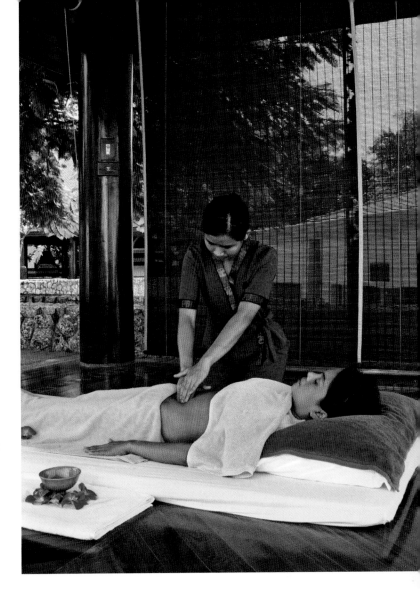

Left: Vibrant Thai silk dominates in the bedroom of this ocean view suite.

Left bottom: Lotus blooms floating on the swimming pool, which faces Hua Hin Beach. The pool bar serves wheatgrass and other healthy juices.

Right: A massage in one of the subtly screened outdoor Thai-style pavilions scattered throughout the beautifully landscaped gardens.

Bottom: Water therapies abound at Chiva-Som, and guests are encouraged to use the Jacuzzi and steam room before or after treatments.

Address: Chiva-Som International Health Resort
73/4 Petchkasem Road
Hua Hin, Prachuab Khirikhan
Thailand
Tel: +66 0 3253 6536
Fax: +66 0 3251 1154
E-mail: reserv@chivasom.com
Website: www.chivasom.com

Left: A converted rice barn amidst the rice paddies is an inspirational setting for yoga.
Above: Filigreed wood-and-brick structures, with steeply pitched multitiered roofs and towers, characterize the residence suites.

Four Seasons Resort Chiang Mai

Secreted away amidst the majestic mountains and lush rice paddies of the Mae Rim Valley, just 20 minutes by road from northern Thailand's fast-growing artistic and cultural capital, Chiang Mai, is the exquisite Four Seasons Resort. Its stunning setting, combined with elegant traditional northern Thai design, attention to detail and personalized service, provide the ultimate base for those looking to explore this northern Thai outpost. Indeed, Chiang Mai is a striking contrast to the country's beach resorts, and the Four Seasons Resort, a self-contained idyllic village, an equally striking contrast to most of the accommodations in this mountainous backwater.

Opened in 1995, the Four Seasons Resort is spread over 20 acres (8 hectares) of landscaped gardens planted with over 200 species of plants and trees, waterways and walkways and, most sensationally, functioning rice paddies (the harvested rice is donated to charity). The resort even shelters a pair of water buffalo that casually wander the property wearing cowbells that clang in the stillness of the afternoon heat, adding an air of pastoral authenticity.

A series of exotic northern Thai-style pavilions, raised on pillars over the landscape, with vaulted ceilings and shingled roofs bearing distinctive gables at the top, are set in clusters of four at the foot of the vast rice fields. Guests can choose from garden,

mountain or rice terrace views. At a massive 750 square feet (70 square meters), the 64 rooms feel more like suites than rooms. Polished teak floors, jewel-toned Thai cottons and silks and exquisite Thai artifacts lend local touches, while spot-lit Thai paintings give each room an art museum quality. The most dramatic feature in each, however, is the huge covered verandah, perfect for viewing the magical scenery, enjoying a room service dinner or relaxing with a book. Housed in more intricate filigreed wood-and-brick buildings, with steeply pitched multitiered roofs, towers and oriels, are the 16 residential suites. These two- or three-bedroom two-story "townhouses" have fabulous interiors and all include special touches such as kitchens, dining rooms, plunge pools and personal housekeepers. The sweeping views of the rice fields, ploughed by buffalo, and the surrounding mountains are unsurpassed. The colors of the fields—and the work done in them—change with the seasons, adding another fascinating dimension for guests.

For those who can pull themselves away from the resort's magnificent infinity-edge swimming pools, with views across the picturesque rice paddies, there are rafting trips, bike trips, tennis, golf, tours of an elephant camp and early morning visits to the local market. Both novice and experienced cooks can also learn "hands on" the art of Thai cuisine at the Cooking School, preparing the dishes and then sampling them in the

Left top and bottom: The spa features seven spacious treatment suites for individuals or couples.

Right: Crisp Chiang Mai mornings are the best time for practicing yoga.

Below: A classic view of terraced rice paddies encircled by ponds and trees.

Above: The two-story pavilion suites, set at the foot of working rice fields, have spacious verandahs and modern amenities.

Left: One of a pair of water buffalo "employed" by the resort to plough the fields.

Opposite top: A series of secluded plunge pools serves several residences.

Opposite bottom: An elephant head at the spa.

Address: Four Seasons
Mae Rim-Samoeng Old Road
Mae Rim, Chiang Mai 50180
Thailand
Tel: +66 0 53 298 181
Fax: +66 0 53 298 190
Website: www.fourseasons.com/chiangmai

open-air dining pavilion, or gain insight into the special Thai art of fruit and vegetable carving. Other guests may prefer more solitary pursuits like practicing yoga in a converted Thai rice barn amidst rice paddies on the outskirts of the resort.

The luxurious three-story spa at the Four Seasons Resort is a sumptuous sanctuary, a special Thai oasis, created exclusively for pampering and well-being. The wide range of treatments, which focus on the use of organic ingredients– local herbs, spices, flowers, fruits and aromatic oils, blended using traditional rural methods–are inspired by ancient Thai rituals.

The unique flavors of northern and vegetarian Thai specialties can be sampled at the high-ceilinged, artifact-filled Sala Mae Rim, located beside the resort's main swimming pool, while international cuisine is available at Terraces.

Mandarin Oriental
Dhara Dhevi Chiang Mai

Described as a "living museum of northern Thai culture," the Dhara Dhevi at Chiang Mai, managed by the Mandarin Oriental, is one of the most ambitious resorts Asia has ever seen. Spread over 60 acres (24 hectares) of serene landscapes incorporating picturesque rice fields, exotic plantations and hardwood forests 15 minutes east of Chiang Mai International Airport, the walled "kingdom" of Dhara Dhevi ("Star Goddess" in Sanskrit) is much more than just another luxury resort. It is a conscious exercise in preserving the amazing architectural heritage and craft styles of the 13th-century northern Thai kingdom of Lanna and the influences it absorbed from its neighbors Myanmar, Laos and China.

More than a dozen ancient architectural styles spanning several centuries are meticulously replicated at Dhara Dhevi in two main time-specific areas. The Lanna "village" encompasses terraced rice paddies worked by resident farmers and buffalo surrounded by two-story guest villas with plunge pools and whirlpool tubs overlooking the paddies, all aristocratically decorated in teak and northern Thai contemporary furnishings and antiques. Narrow lanes meander through the village to the hotel's restaurants offering French, Thai and Chinese cuisine, the shopping arcade

Opposite top and bottom: The luxurious Dheva
Spa, located in a cluster of Burmese-style teak
buildings, focuses on treatments unique to
Thailand, beginning with a welcoming foot ritual.
Above: View from the spa's penthouse suite.

Left: Pounding *thanaka*, a yellowish-white paste made from the bark of several trees, for use as a cooling cosmetic and gentle body scrub.

Below and opposite top left and right: The entrance (below) and the seven-tiered teakwood roof (opposite top left) of the 33,368 square foot (3,100 square meter) Dheva Spa are modeled on the former Royal Palace at Mandalay, Myanmar.

Opposite bottom: Intricately decorated multi-colored Thai Bencharong ware on display in a perforated wall at the entrance to the spa treatment rooms.

selling locally made goods out of shuttered wooden shophouses, the Oriental Culinary Academy, and the sumptuous Dheva Spa, housed in a magnificent re-creation of a 19th-century Burmese palace capped by a seven-tier roof, which offers treatments inspired by both Thai and Burmese cultures. A bridge across a waterway leads to the second, colonial, section, where spacious theme suites sport chandeliers, tiled bathrooms and 1920s Shanghai-style Chinese accents. The grounds are so vast that guests move around on bicycles or electric golf carts or in horse-drawn carriages. Apart from sporting activities, or simply gazing at farmers harvesting rice from the two infinity-edge pools, a variety of educational, art and culture activities are available at Dhara Dhevi.

Left and above: Teak and bamboo furniture and northern Thai textiles, basketware and carvings add panache to the two-story villas.
Below: Colonial charm in the spa's penthouse suite.
Opposite top: The terraced rice paddies are farmed by blue-shirted farmers and resident water buffalo.
Opposite bottom: The open-air Farang Ses restaurant overlooks rice paddies and coconut palms.

Address: Mandarin Oriental Dhara Dhevi Chiang Mai
51/4 Chiang Mai-Sankampaeng Road
Moo 1 T. Tasala A. Muang
Chiang Mai 50000, Thailand
Tel: +66 53 888 888
Fax: +66 53 888 999
E-mail: mocnx-reservations@mohg.com
Website: www.mandarinoriental.com/chiangmai

Rayavadee Krabi

Rayavadee's setting at the heart of the stunning Phranang Peninsula on the edge of the Krabi National Marine Park, about 500 miles (800 km) south of Bangkok, adds considerably to its allure. The resort is flanked on three sides by powdery white sand beaches crowned by soaring jungle-clad limestone cliffs pocked with caverns and caves, and the reef-dotted emerald waters of the Andaman Sea. Although Krabi Airport has numerous daily flights from Bangkok and Phuket International Airport is a mere two-hour drive away, Rayavadee is accessible only by boat from Krabi Town, making the luxurious resort accessible yet still intensely private. Guests are whisked away from Krabi on the resort's private speedboat manned by uniformed staff for a dizzying 35-minute spin before shimmying into one of the resort's three bays.

Inspired by the atmosphere of a southern Thai village, Rayavadee has 98 two-story pavilions, some with private gardens, barbecue terraces, hydro pools and outdoor Jacuzzis, and four beachfront villas with private pools, spread over 26 acres (10 hectares) of coconut groves nestled beneath spectacular, almost vertical cliffs. All have bathtubs for two and snuggly cushioned wooden swings instead of sofas. The pavilions and villas are distinctive for their mushroom-shaped roofs, sandy-colored exteriors and muted interiors.

A huge swimming pool seemingly melts into the Andaman Sea and is a showpiece of Rayavadee although most guests prefer to spend lazy days on one of the three idyllic beaches surrounding the resort. For the more active, Rayavadee offers a host of non-motorized water sports—canoeing, snorkeling, sailing, laser boarding, scuba diving and fishing—as well as rock climbing, excursions on a restored Siamese junk to uninhabited islands in the marine reserve and treks in the lush forested interior, including a steep climb up a limestone cliff to look down upon Princess Lagoon.

Left: One of the fantastical lime-stone cliffs to explore at the beaches near Rayavadee.
Above: An exotic tropical bloom.
Below: The serene Rayavadee Spa offers uniquely Thai treatments.
Right: The large lagoon-style infinity pool, encircled by verdant landscaped gardens, lies between the mushroom-like pavilions at the base of the cliff and the sea.
Opposite bottom: A bedroom in Phranang Villa is decorated in tropical tones.

Five specialty restaurants, running a delectable gamut of flavors from Thai to international cuisines, are enough to satisfy any palate. The most scenic of them, The Grotto, is cleft into the cliffside and carpeted with a cool layer of sand. There are also numerous independent cafés, beach restaurants and eateries on Railay Beach for those seeking an alternative to hotel fare.

The Rayavadee Spa offers full beauty and spa facilities. Therapeutic Thai herbal ingredients, masterful masseurs, an extensive menu of Thai massages, scrubs, wraps, facials and baths and a soothing ambience are reason to spend time there.

Nearby attractions include Phi Phi and Bamboo Islands, which can be reached in 35 minutes by speedboat from the resort. Apart from their white sands, crystal-blue waters and jagged cliffs, the reefs surrounding them are home to a great variety of tropical fish and marine life. Closer still, Poda, Chicken and Tub Islands, with their lovely beaches and strange rock formations, are perfect for half-day excursions. As most people in Krabi earn their living from farming and fishing, Krabi Town's vibrant market offers a glimpse of traditional local life.

Above: Local youths hang off craggy cliffs.

Above right: Rayavadee Villa has its own free-form pool with an inbuilt Jacuzzi.

Below: The brilliant colours of tropical trees.

Right: A blossom-filled Jacuzzi at the spa demonstrates the artistry of the Thai.

Opposite: A view from the reception area.

Address: Rayavadee
214 Moo 2, Tambon Ao-Nang
Amphoe Muang
Krabi 81000, Thailand
Tel: +66 75 620 740
Fax: +66 75 620 630
E-mail: reservation@rayavadee.com
Website: www.rayavadee.com

The Peninsula Bangkok

Opened in May 1999, The Peninsula in Bangkok quickly established itself as one of the city's classiest hotels for its prime location, architectural and interior finishes, landscaping, amenities, hospitality and service. Thanks to its unique "W"-shaped design and location on the west bank of Bangkok's scenic Chao Phraya River, guests in every one of the 39-story hotel's large rooms or suites can enjoy uninterrupted panoramic views of the fascinating river life below and the teeming city beyond. A 10-minute ride on one of the hotel's charming shuttle boats takes guests across the river to Bangkok's major attractions and shopping, nightlife and business areas.

In addition to the marble finishes, plush carpets, high ceilings and sweeping staircases in the public areas, each of the guest rooms and suites is appointed to reflect the perfect marriage of Thai tradition and high-tech luxury.

For relaxation at the hotel, there is an impressive 196-foot (60-meter) three-tiered swimming pool lined with *sala*, little teak-roofed pavilions, and sundeck areas for an escape from the sun, or the luxurious Peninsula Spa, opened in December 2006 in a restored Thai colonial-style house adjacent to the Fitness centre, which offers the ultimate in wellness programs by skilled therapists in its 18 treatment rooms and suites. The hotel's elegant and chic dining options have the same classy Peninsula touch, and range from contemporary Pacific Rim cuisine to authentic Thai and Cantonese.

Address: The Peninsula Bangkok
333 Charoen Nakhorn Road
Klongsan, Bangkok 10600
Thailand
Tel: +66 2 861 2888
Fax: +66 2 861 1112
E-mail: pbk@peninsula.com
Website: www.peninsula.com/Bangkok

Opposite top: Wood paneling, silk wallpaper, plush seating and thick carpets spell timeless elegance in the hotel's suites. High ceilings and full-length windows with unfettered views add to the luxury of space.

Opposite bottom left and right, and right: The open-air River Café & Terrace offers guests an extensive international buffet.

Below: The 5,800 sq ft (1,770 sq m) spa is part of the "Peninsula Wellness" program.

The Tongsai Bay
Koh Samui

One of the few resorts on the Gulf of Thailand's paradise island of Koh Samui with its own private beach, the laid-back and eco-friendly Tongsai Bay resort is wonderfully located in the quiet northeastern part of the island, a mere 10 minutes' drive from Koh Samui Airport. Blending harmoniously with its surroundings, the resort slopes gently down a hillside to meet the perfect 660-foot (200-meter)-long, horseshoe-shaped Choengmon Beach, enclosed on each side by hills that taper down to rocky headlands. There is an emphasis on open space, sun and sea, with none of the overcrowding, overbuilding and overplanting, especially of coconut palms, seen in so many beachside resorts. Trees and rocks on the site were carefully preserved during construction. The undisturbed habitat has meant that 40 species of birds continue to enjoy the resort's verdant surroundings.

The 25-acre (10 hectare) site is home to a variety of accommodations, including beachfront suites housed in a striking teak-and-glass three-story building facing the sea and close to the main swimming pool and, flanking it, semidetached split-level cottage suites, the ones on the ground floor with direct access to the pool; and on the opposite hill at the end of the beach, several stylish and more recently built Tongsai grand villas and pool villas. All 83 rooms at the resort have spacious wooden verandahs or terraces furnished with sun loungers and bathtubs which offer superb sea views. The largest of the villas can accommodate canopied beds on their verandahs for outdoor sleeping as well as tubs for lazy soaks.

Two large swimming pools complement dips in the azure ocean, one a large, roundish, free-form pool very close to the beach, and the

Above and left: This Tongsai grand villa, high up on a hill, boasts a romantic canopied bed and a bath-with-a-view on its spacious private verandah.
Opposite: The holistic Prana Spa offers relaxing massages and body treatments.

other a stunning half-moon pool with an infinity-edge further up the slope for quieter swims, where no children are allowed. There are also non-motorized water sports such as sailing, windsurfing, snorkeling and canoeing for the more energetic, as well as tennis, working out in the gym and a range of beach activities.

A stay at The Tongsai Bay would not be complete without a visit to the resort's holistic spa, Prana. Treatments encompass everything from aromatherapy to traditional Thai massage, body masks and Dead Sea mud therapies.

Gastronomic options are also varied. Three restaurants are open for dinner and each presents weekly theme nights. Chef Chom's Thai restaurant provides an opportunity for guests to indulge in authentic royal Thai cuisine as well as local southern food. A more intimate outlet, The Butler's Restaurant, overlooking the half-moon swimming pool and the sea offers a European menu to a backdrop of live music and shows. It seats 20 adult only diners. Floyd's Beach Bistro with bar, named after British television chef Keith Floyd who helped the owner plan the concept, is conveniently located on the beachfront next to the pool and is a popular gathering place. It serves international food with a contemporary touch as well as snacks in an alfresco setting. The glass-fronted, air-conditioned Sip Internet Café offers a range of coffee blends and treats. Night owls can party the night away—or at least until 2 a.m.—at the Beach Bar. With views straight onto the beach and over the bay, these are favorite venues for guests to relax and enjoy themselves. The hotel's management also hosts twice-weekly cocktail parties, giving guests an opportunity to mingle over drinks.

Top: The main pool located near the beach.
Above: On the pathway leading to the stylish Prana Spa.
Opposite top right: The Butler's Restaurant, adjacent to the half-moon pool, serves European food.
Opposite top left: Spa materials.
Opposite bottom: The view from Chef Chom's Thai restaurant.

Address: The Tongsai Bay

84 Moo 5, Bo Phut

Koh Samui, Surat Thani 84320

Thailand

Tel: +66 77 245 480

Fax: +66 77 425 462

E-mail: reservation@tongsaibay.co.th

Website: www.tongsaibay.co.th

One & Only Royal Mirage Dubai

The One & Only Royal Mirage Hotel in Dubai, capital of the United Arab Emirates, is imbued with the essence of Arabian architecture and hospitality on a grand scale. Strategically located 20 minutes from Dubai International Airport on a private section of the exclusive Jumeira Beach overlooking the Arabian Sea, opposite the prestigious Emirates Golf Club and adjacent to the Dubai International Marine Club, the stylish property, opened in 1999, comprises three distinctive and separate hotels: the original hotel (the Palace), the Arabian Court and the Residence & Spa. The Residence, comprising three secluded villas, 18 suites and 32 deluxe rooms and its own reception, lounge and restaurant, also houses the Oriental Hammam & Spa, notewothy for its impressive architecture-towering domes, arches and intricate carvings-and treatments.

Scenes from the Arabian Nights greet guests as they enter the grand gallery, the vertebrae of the One & Only Royal Mirage that links the two wings and guides guests toward their choice of accommodation from the 246 lavishly appointed deluxe rooms or suites available, all with views of the sea from private balconies or ground-floor patios.

The Arabian-themed architecture is apparent every-where-in the arches, colonnades and porches, the inter-laced geometric patterning on arches, and the ornamental motifs and mosaics on walls, floors and ceilings-comple-mented by sumptuous soft furnishings and lighting. The

60 acres (24 hectares) of gardens encompassing the resort are framed and integrated with the architecture. Beautifully landscaped in the Islamic tradition with formal, geometric courtyards, water features and pathways, the gardens blend tradition with fantasy in the opulent splendor of this rediscovered Arabian "fortress."

The hotel's many dining rooms and bars follow Arabian themes, among them the Kasbar Bar, Olives Restaurant and Samovar Lounge, and offer a variety of food and beverages, much of which is imported. Leisure facilities include swimming pools and a water sports center as well as the impressive Oriental Hammam & Spa, located within the Residence, where guests are pampered within a traditional setting.

Left top: A corner of the lobby at the Arabian Court.

Left bottom: An elegantly appointed guest room at the Arabian Court.

Above: A glimpse of the intricately painted domed ceiling in the entrance lobby of the Palace, the original hotel.

Right: The Givenchy Spa in the Residence & Spa.

Below: A table tiled with Islamic motifs beside the pool.

Left: The hotel offers a comprehensive range of water sports at the exclusive Jumeira Beach, which looks out over the Arabian Gulf.
Below: A view of the symmetrical palm-flanked lap pool from the Arabian Court.
Opposite: Tradition and fantasy blend in the brilliant painted domed ceiling of the entrance lobby to the Palace.

Address: One & Only Royal Mirage
PO Box 37252, Dubai
United Arab Emirates
Tel: +971 4 399 99 99
Fax: +971 4 399 99 98
E-mail: info@oneandonly-royalmirage.ae
Website: www.oneandonly-royalmirage.com

Acknowledgments

I would like to extend a big "thank you" to the management and staff of all the *ryokan* and resorts that are featured in this book. Without their assistance, hospitality and patience, it would not have been possible for me and my team to visit, experience, photograph and learn about these wonderful places. A special thank you also goes to Asako, Kaoruko, Akio and Yukiko for their help and companionship over the years. I would also like to acknowledge Yuichi Yoshino of Laseed Inc., who published *The Resort Kingdom*, my first book on Asia's wonderful resorts, and Eric Oey of Periplus Editions for publishing this new edition. Special thanks to Noor Azlina Yunus for helping to rewrite and improve the text of this book.